Contents

Theme 4 **Animal Habitats**

Selection Connections 1

Nights of the Pufflings 3

Reading-Writing Workshop:
A Research Report 18

Seal Surfer 23

Two Days in May 38

Monitoring Student Progress 53

Connecting and Comparing Literature . . . 53

Preparing for Tests 57

Focus on Biography 68

Theme 5 **Voyagers**

Selection Connections 83

Across the Wide Dark Sea 85

Reading-Writing Workshop:
Description 100

Yunmi and Halmoni's Trip 105

Trapped by the Ice! 120

Monitoring Student Progress 135

Connecting and Comparing Literature . . . 135

Preparing for Tests 139

Focus on Fairy Tales 150

Contents

Theme 6 Smart Solutions

Selection Connections 165

Pepita Talks Twice 167

Reading-Writing Workshop:

A Persuasive Essay 182

Poppa's New Pants 187

Ramona Quimby, Age 8 202

Monitoring Student Progress 217

Connecting and Comparing Literature . . . 217

Preparing for Tests 221

Student Handbook 233

Spelling 235

How to Study a Word

Words Often Misspelled

Take-Home Word Lists

Grammar and Usage: Problem Words . . 249

Proofreading Checklist 250

Proofreading Marks 251

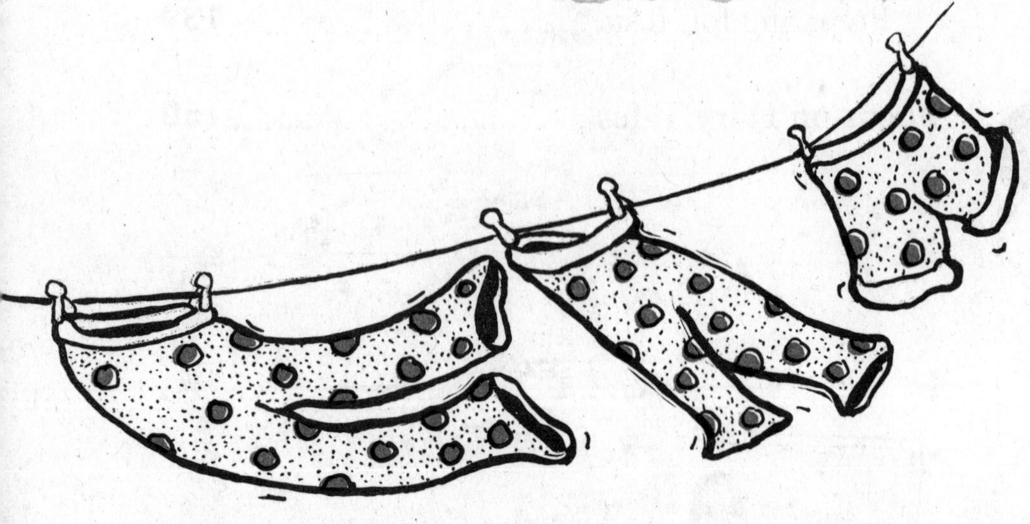

Name ____________________

Animal Habitats

Draw a picture of an animal on this page. Then answer the questions.

1. What do you think this animal needs in order to live?

____

____

2. In what kinds of places do you think this animal could live?

____

____

3. What do you like best about this animal? Why?

____

____

Name ______________________________

Animal Habitats

As you read each selection in Animal Habitats, fill in the boxes of the chart that apply to the selection.

	How do the people and animals meet?	What happens when the people and animals meet?
Nights of the Pufflings		
Seal Surfer		
Two Days in May		

Name ______________________________

Bird Words

Write the correct word next to each definition. Then find and circle all seven words in the word search.

ashore
burrows
instinctively
launching
stranded
uninhabited
venture

1. Holes animals use as underground nests.

   ____

2. To do something risky. ______________________________
3. Sending upwards like a rocket. ______________________________
4. On or to the shore. ______________________________
5. Acting on a feeling, without thinking. ______________________________
6. Having no people living there. ______________________________
7. Stuck or trapped. ______________________________

I	N	S	T	I	N	C	T	I	V	E	L	Y
W	P	U	N	I	N	H	A	B	I	T	E	D
G	N	L	N	R	T	O	N	Q	M	R	G	L
W	V	A	L	P	V	E	N	T	U	R	E	A
K	P	A	S	H	O	R	E	W	O	T	J	U
B	B	P	H	A	X	D	E	J	L	I	Y	N
E	K	U	S	A	J	U	X	V	B	M	R	C
C	W	K	R	B	N	B	S	W	G	S	U	H
C	V	S	T	R	A	N	D	E	D	R	D	I
R	O	J	A	X	O	Q	T	S	G	K	C	N
Q	W	M	M	O	D	W	R	Q	I	C	A	G
I	N	S	A	F	P	A	S	Y	C	R	C	B

Name ______________________________

Puffin Fact Chart

Why Puffins Come to the Island (page 21)	What Growing Puffin Chicks Do (page 25)
1. ____________________ ____________________ ____________________ 2. ____________________ ____________________ ____________________	1. ____________________ ____________________ 2. ____________________ ____________________ 3. ____________________ ____________________
What Puffins Look Like and What They Do (pages 22–23)	**What Happens on Pufflings' First Flight to the Sea (pages 28–32)**
1. ____________________ ____________________ 2. ____________________ ____________________ 3. ____________________ ____________________ 4. ____________________ ____________________	1. ____________________ ____________________ 2. ____________________ ____________________ 3. ____________________ ____________________ 4. ____________________ ____________________

Name ______________________________

The Problem with Pufflings

Finish each sentence about *Nights of the Pufflings.*

1. After a winter at sea, puffins return to Halla's island because

   ____

2. Halla and her friends can't see the baby chicks because

   ____

3. In August, the young pufflings come out of their burrows because

   ____

4. Pufflings that don't make it to the ocean are in danger because

   ____

5. The children wander through the streets at night because

   ____

6. The next day the children take their cardboard boxes to the beach because

   ____

Name ______________________________

Fact or Opinion?

Read the story. Then go on to the next page.

A Bird by Any Other Name

Another name for a pigeon is a rock dove, and, indeed, pigeons belong to the same bird family as doves. Doves are thought to be clean, pretty, and gentle. But pigeons really look very dirty. They can be messy too!

If you live in a city, you've probably seen lots of them in parks and other places where people eat their lunch. To find food, pigeons will make pests of themselves. In some cities the return of falcons and hawks has cut down on pigeon numbers. Be glad that there are fewer pigeons around!

Some people train pigeons to fly home from many miles away. These pigeons are known as homing pigeons. They can carry messages. Scientists think that sunlight and Earth's magnetism help the pigeons know where to fly.

In the early 1800s, millions of passenger pigeons lived in North America. As settlers moved west, they hunted the birds for meat, fat, and feathers. By 1880, most passenger pigeons were gone. The last one died in a zoo in 1914. It's sad to think there are no more passenger pigeons.

Name ______________________________

Fact or Opinion? continued

Read each statement below. Decide if it is a fact or opinion. Write *fact* or *opinion* on the line.

1. Another name for a pigeon is a rock dove. ______________
2. Pigeons belong to the same family of birds as doves. ______________
3. Pigeons are really very dirty birds. ______________
4. You can see pigeons in parks. ______________
5. Pigeons make pests of themselves. ______________
6. You should be glad that there are fewer pigeons around. ______________
7. Homing pigeons can carry messages. ______________
8. The last passenger pigeon died in 1914. ______________
9. It's sad that there are no more passenger pigeons. ______________

How did you figure out which of the statements above were opinions? Write a sentence to explain your thinking.

____

____

Name ______________________________

Dictionary Disaster

The writers of this dictionary page need your help. They have included each word, its part of speech, and its definition. Now finish each entry by dividing the word into syllables.

Example: notebook *noun* A book with blank pages to write on.

note • book

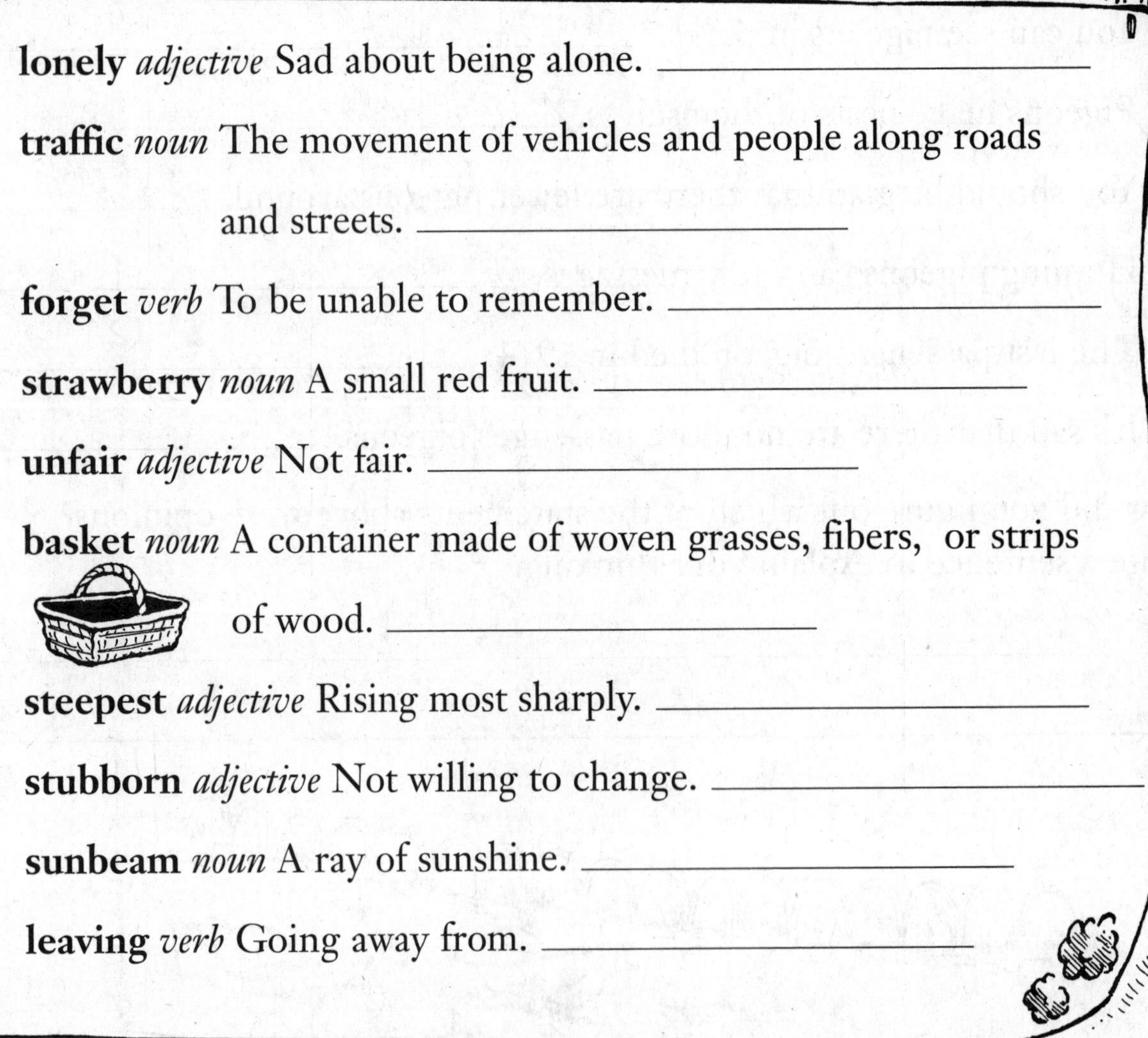

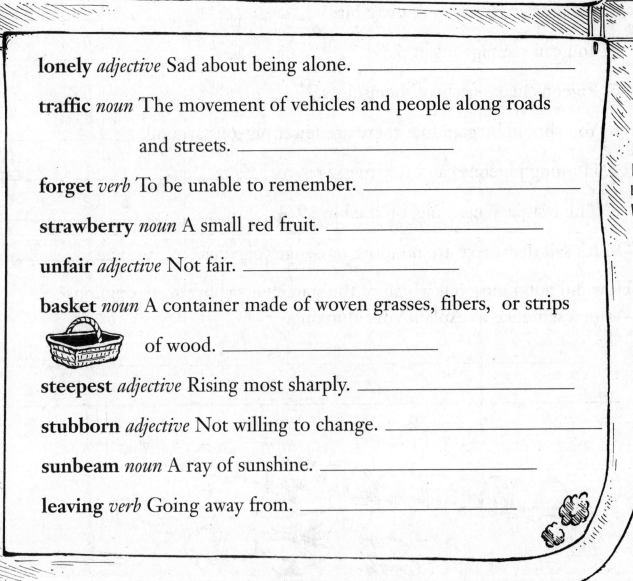

lonely *adjective* Sad about being alone. ______________________________

traffic *noun* The movement of vehicles and people along roads and streets. ______________________________

forget *verb* To be unable to remember. ______________________________

strawberry *noun* A small red fruit. ______________________________

unfair *adjective* Not fair. ______________________________

basket *noun* A container made of woven grasses, fibers, or strips of wood. ______________________________

steepest *adjective* Rising most sharply. ______________________________

stubborn *adjective* Not willing to change. ______________________________

sunbeam *noun* A ray of sunshine. ______________________________

leaving *verb* Going away from. ______________________________

Name ______________________________

The Vowel + /r/ Sounds in *hair*

Spelling Words

1. hair
2. care
3. chair
4. pair
5. bear
6. where*
7. scare
8. air
9. pear
10. bare
11. fair
12. share

There are three different ways to spell the /âr/ sounds heard in *hair.* The three patterns are as follows:

are, as in c**are**
air, as in h**air**
ear, as in b**ear**

► In the starred word *where*, the /âr/ sounds are spelled *ere.*

Write each Spelling Word under its spelling of the /âr/ sounds.

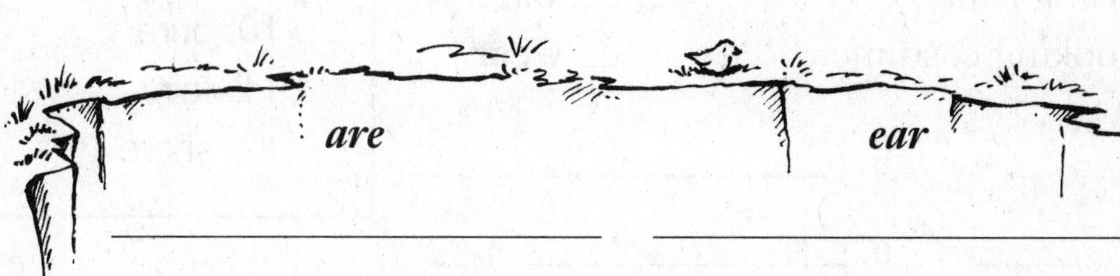

are

____

____

____

____

ear

____

____

Another Spelling

____

air

____

____

____

____

____

Name ______________________________

Spelling Spree

Hink Pinks Write the Spelling Word that fits the clue and rhymes with the given word.

Example: a purchase during an airplane flight **sky** buy

1. a long look by a large, furry animal ____ **stare**
2. a rip in a seat cushion ____ **tear**
3. a hairless rabbit ____ **hare**
4. taking care of a female horse **mare** ____
5. products made from animal fur ____ **ware**
6. a challenge to eat a fruit ____ **dare**
7. a frightening-looking costume ____ **wear**

1. ______________ 5. ______________

2. ______________ 6. ______________

3. ______________ 7. ______________

4. ______________

Spelling Words

1. hair
2. care
3. chair
4. pair
5. bear
6. where*
7. scare
8. air
9. pear
10. bare
11. fair
12. share

Letter Swap Change the underlined letter in each word to make a Spelling Word. Write the Spelling Word.

Example: would *could*

8. fail ______________ 11. fir ______________

9. there ______________ 12. paid ______________

10. shape ______________

Name ______________________________

Proofreading and Writing

Proofreading Circle the five misspelled Spelling Words. Then write each word correctly.

Spelling Words

1. hair
2. care
3. chair
4. pair
5. bear
6. where*
7. scare
8. air
9. pear
10. bare
11. fair
12. share

Iceland at a Glance

Iceland is an island in the Atlantic Ocean. Most visitors arrive by aer. Few travel to the center of the island, whare glaciers cover most of the land. Even the coastal areas are almost bair of trees. The people of Iceland take kare to make visitors feel welcome. They are happy to shear their favorite foods with you. If you go to this unusual island, you'll enjoy your visit!

1. ____________________
2. ____________________
3. ____________________
4. ____________________
5. ____________________

Write a Notice The children of Heimaey Island do their best to rescue the lost pufflings. You want to help by writing a notice warning people to watch out for the young birds. How would you get people's attention? What would you ask them to do?

On a separate sheet of paper, write a notice to the people of Heimaey Island. Use Spelling Words from the list.

Name ______________________________

Name the Part of Speech

Read each sentence. Decide the part of speech for each underlined word. Then choose the correct meaning. Write the correct letter in the blank.

1. Halla spots her first puffin of the season. _____
   a. *noun* Small marks or stains.
   b. *verb* Finds or locates.

2. The puffins land while the children are in school. _____
   a. *noun* The part of Earth not covered by water.
   b. *verb* To come down on a surface.

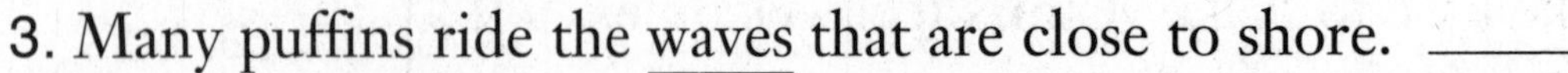

3. Many puffins ride the waves that are close to shore. _____
   a. *noun* Ridges or swells moving across a body of water.
   b. *verb* Flaps or flutters.

4. Halla's friend spies a puffin overhead. _____
   a. *noun* Secret agents who get information about an enemy.
   b. *verb* Catches sight of; sees.

5. The pufflings cannot take off from flat ground. _____
   a. *noun* The solid surface of the earth; land.
   b. *verb* To cause to touch the bottom of a body of water.

6. Halla wishes the little birds a safe journey. _____
   a. *noun* A trip; a passage from one place to another.
   b. *verb* To make a journey.

Name ______________________________

Completing with *be*

Complete each sentence. Fill in the blank with the form of *be* that matches the subject. Use the tense named in parentheses.

1. The story ____________ about pufflings. (present)
2. We ____________ curious about these birds. (present)
3. The pufflings ____________ beautiful. (past)
4. Halla ____________ ready. (past)
5. She ____________ very clever. (present)
6. The birds ____________ confused by the village lights. (present)
7. Children ____________ everywhere, searching for lost birds. (past)
8. One small puffling ____________ stranded in the village. (past)
9. The students ____________ very brave. (past)
10. I ____________ glad they rescued the pufflings. (present)

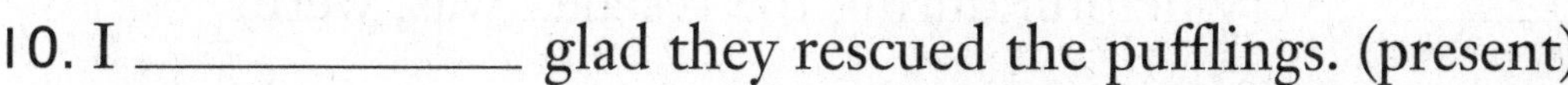

Name ______________________

Be-ing Smart

The Irregular Verb *be*		
Subject	**Present**	**Past**
I	am	was
you	are	were
he, she, it, singular noun	is	was
we, they	are	were
plural noun	are	were

Use the verbs in the chart to complete these sentences. Cross off each verb in the chart when you use it.

1. The puffin ____________ a beautiful bird. (am, is)
2. I ____________ sorry that some get stranded. (am, are)
3. You ____________ very helpful during the rescue. (was, were)
4. The students ____________ heroes. (are, am)
5. We ____________ surprised by the number of pufflings. (was, were)
6. I ____________ almost frightened by the strange noises. (was, were)
7. The puffling's cry ____________ sad. (were, was)
8. The young birds ____________ hungry. (was, were)
9. You ____________ curious about pufflings. (is, are)
10. They ____________ fascinating animals. (are, is)

Name ______________________________

Forms of the Verb *be*

Good writers are careful to use the correct form of the verb *be*. When the verb is correct, the subject of the sentence and the verb match.

Rewrite the postcard. Correct the forms of *be*.

Dear Elena,

Hello from Iceland. You was right! This vacation were really amazing. The pufflings is the cutest birds.

We was outside one night. We heard a small cry. The sound be very sad. It be a little peep-peep-peep.

Two little pufflings was stranded in the street. We caught them in a box. The night were very cold, but we didn't care. We let the birds go at the beach. They was so happy near the ocean. We was happy too.

See you soon,
Marcia

____

____

____

____

____

____

____

____

____

____

Name ______________________________

Taking Notes

Read this passage to find out more about Iceland.

ICELAND

N

The Land of the Midnight Sun

Iceland is a country that is also a large island. It is very far north, close to the Arctic Circle, in the North Atlantic Ocean. For two months in the winter, it is dark all the time, except for four to six hours of light a day. But in June, it is daylight all the time. There is no night at all. That is why Iceland is called "The Land of the Midnight Sun."

Even though Iceland is very far north, it is not as cold as you might expect. Most people in Iceland live on the coast. Warm winds from the sea keep the coast from getting very cold. The winters are mild compared to the winters in the northern United States and Canada. The summers in Iceland are cool. The temperature is more like spring than the hot summers most Americans and Canadians are used to.

Take notes on the passage and write them in the outline below.

Iceland

What is it? ______________________________

Where is it? ______________________________

Why is it called "The Land of the Midnight Sun"? ______________________________

____

____

What is the weather like? ______________________________

____

Name ______________________

Choosing What's Important

Read this passage. Then answer the questions below.

Natural Wonders of Iceland

The inner part of Iceland has few people but many wonders of nature.

Volcanoes A volcano is an opening in the earth over very hot melted rock. It gives off a gas that pushes up through the opening and makes a big explosion. *Iceland has over 200 volcanoes.*

Geysers Geysers are hot springs that throw streams of water into the air. The word *geyser* comes from *Geysir,* the most famous natural fountain in Iceland.

A trip to Iceland would show you many wonders of nature.

1. What do the two subheadings tell about the title?

____

2. Look at the last sentence under "Volcanoes." Why do you think it is in slanted letters? ______________________

____

3. Which two words appear in slanted type under "Geysers"? Why?

____

4. What does the picture show? ______________________

____

5. What information is repeated in the last paragraph? ______________________

____

Name ______________________________

Revising Your Research Report

Reread your report. Put a checkmark in the box for each sentence that describes your paper. Use this page to help you revise.

Rings the Bell

- ☐ My report is focused on one topic. I did a lot of research.
- ☐ Paragraphs have main ideas that are supported by facts.
- ☐ I wrote the facts in my own words. I used exact words.
- ☐ The conclusion sums up my report. I included a complete list of sources.
- ☐ My sentences flow well. There are few mistakes.

Getting Stronger

- ☐ The report could be more focused. I need more facts.
- ☐ My paragraphs need topic sentences or supporting facts.
- ☐ I did not always write in my own words. More exact words are needed.
- ☐ The conclusion is weak. The list of sources is incomplete.
- ☐ Some sentences are choppy. There are some mistakes.

Try Harder

- ☐ I never focused on a topic. There are almost no facts.
- ☐ My facts are not organized in paragraphs.
- ☐ I copied sentences from a source. There are no exact words.
- ☐ The conclusion and the list of sources are missing.
- ☐ Most sentences are choppy. There are many mistakes.

Name ____________________

Subject-Verb Agreement

Circle the correct form of each verb.

1. Lizards (is/are) the largest group in the reptile family.
2. The Komodo dragon (is/are) the largest lizard.
3. The Komodo dragon (measure/measures) up to 10 feet in length.
4. Lizards (lives/live) in every kind of habitat except the ocean.
5. All reptiles (are/is) cold-blooded.
6. A cold-blooded animal (do/does) not make its own body heat.
7. To warm its blood, a lizard (bask/basks) in the sun.
8. I (own/owns) a lizard called a swift.
9. The swift (move/moves) slowly when it is cold.
10. Then I (turn/turns) on a heat lamp.
11. Suddenly, the swift (runs/run) very fast.
12. At night, lizards (hide/hides) to stay away from enemies.

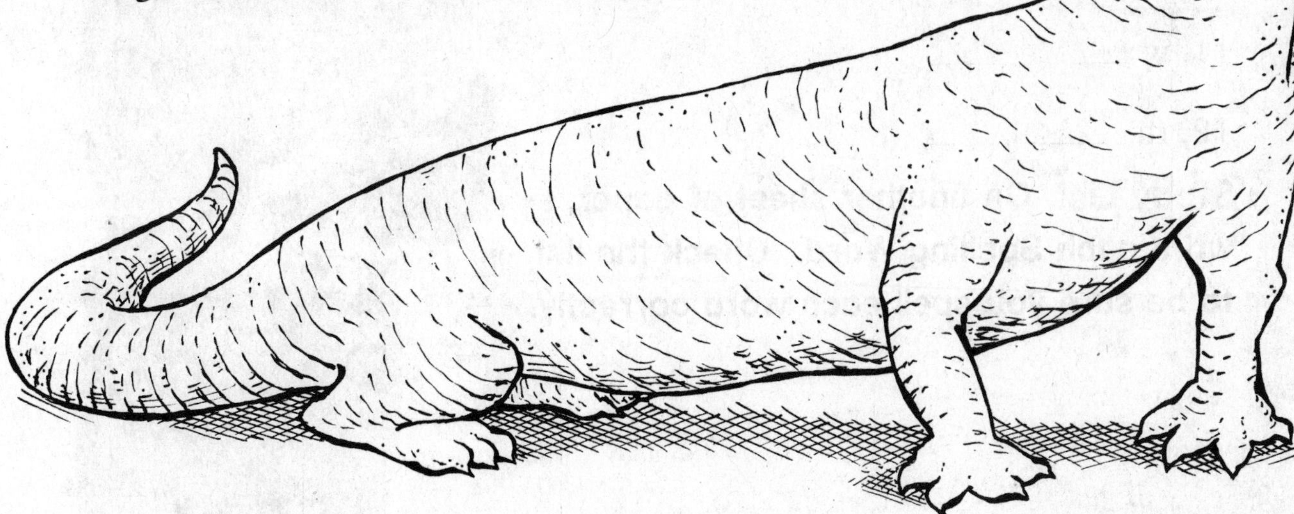

Name ______________________________

Spelling Words

Look for spelling patterns you have learned to help you remember the Spelling Words on this page. Think about the parts that you find hard to spell.

Write the missing letters in the Spelling Words below.

1. c ___ ___ ___ d
2. ___ lot
3. b ___ y
4. ___ ___ r
5. w ___ ___ ___ d
6. n ___ ___
7. ___ ___ o
8. g ___ ___ l
9. w ___ nt
10. in ___ ___
11. w ___ ___
12. th ___ ___

Study List **On another sheet of paper, write each Spelling Word. Check the list to be sure you spell each word correctly.**

Spelling Words

1. girl
2. they
3. want
4. was
5. into
6. who
7. our
8. new
9. would
10. could
11. a lot
12. buy

Name ______________________________

Reading-Writing Workshop
Frequently Misspelled Words

Spelling Spree

Opposites Switch **Write the Spelling Word that means the opposite of each underlined word or words.**

1–2. I wouldn't be able to run much faster if I couldn't find a pair of shoes that fit.
3–4. The old parents named their baby boy Sue.
5–6. It takes a little of money to sell a boat that big.
7–8. I wasn't going out of the park when I saw smoke coming from a nearby house.

1–2. ______________________________
3–4. ______________________________
5–6. ______________________________
7–8. ______________________________

Spelling Words

1. girl
2. they
3. want
4. was
5. into
6. who
7. our
8. new
9. would
10. could
11. a lot
12. buy

Letter Math **Add and subtract letters from the words below to make Spelling Words. Write the new words.**

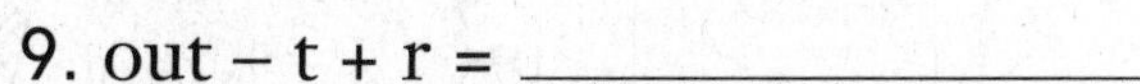

9. out – t + r = ______________
10. then – n + y = ______________
11. while – ile + o = ______________
12. slant – sl + w = ______________

Reading-Writing Workshop

Frequently Misspelled Words

Name ______________________________

Proofreading and Writing

Proofreading Circle the four misspelled Spelling Words in this announcement. Then write each word correctly.

The State Zoo is proud to announce a noo approach to exhibiting our animals. Each animal's home is now more like the habitat thay would find in the wild. We think that the change will make alot of difference in the lives of the animals. And after all, we wont the animals to feel that this is their home!

Spelling Words

1. girl
2. they
3. want
4. was
5. into
6. who
7. our
8. new
9. would
10. could
11. a lot
12. buy

1. ______________ 3. ______________

2. ______________ 4. ______________

Describe a Habitat Draw a picture of an animal in its habitat. Then write a few sentences describing what you drew. The animal can be real or imaginary. Use Spelling Words from the list.

Name ______________________________

Beach Crossword

Complete the crossword puzzle using the words from the box.

Vocabulary

basked
buffeted
horizon
quay
surf
swell
seal
swooped

Across

2. a dock
3. dived downward
4. rested in warmth
6. a long, rolling wave
7. the line where earth and sky meet

Down

1. struck against powerfully
5. sea animal with fur and flippers
6. waves, or to ride on waves

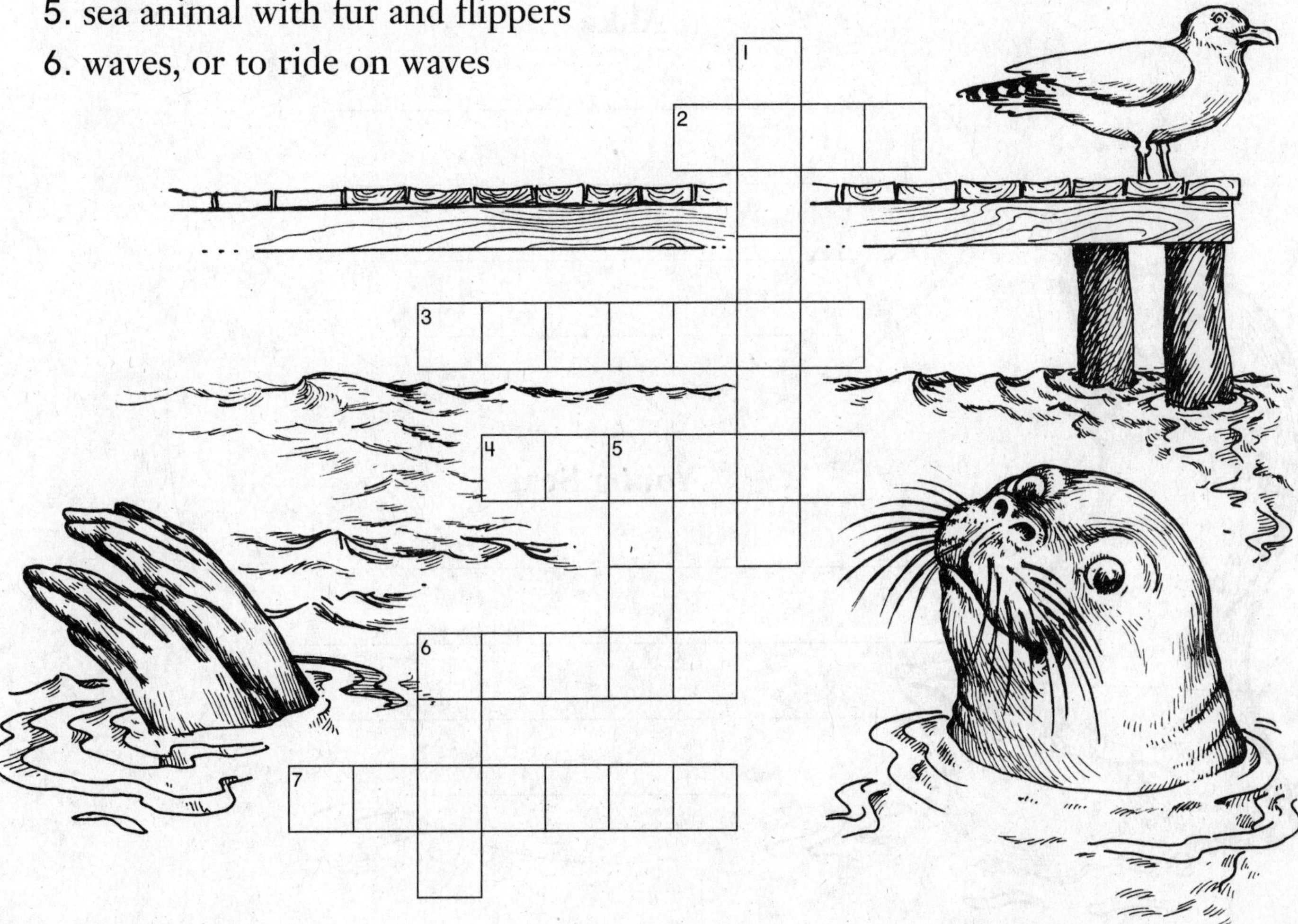

Name ______________________________

Venn Diagram

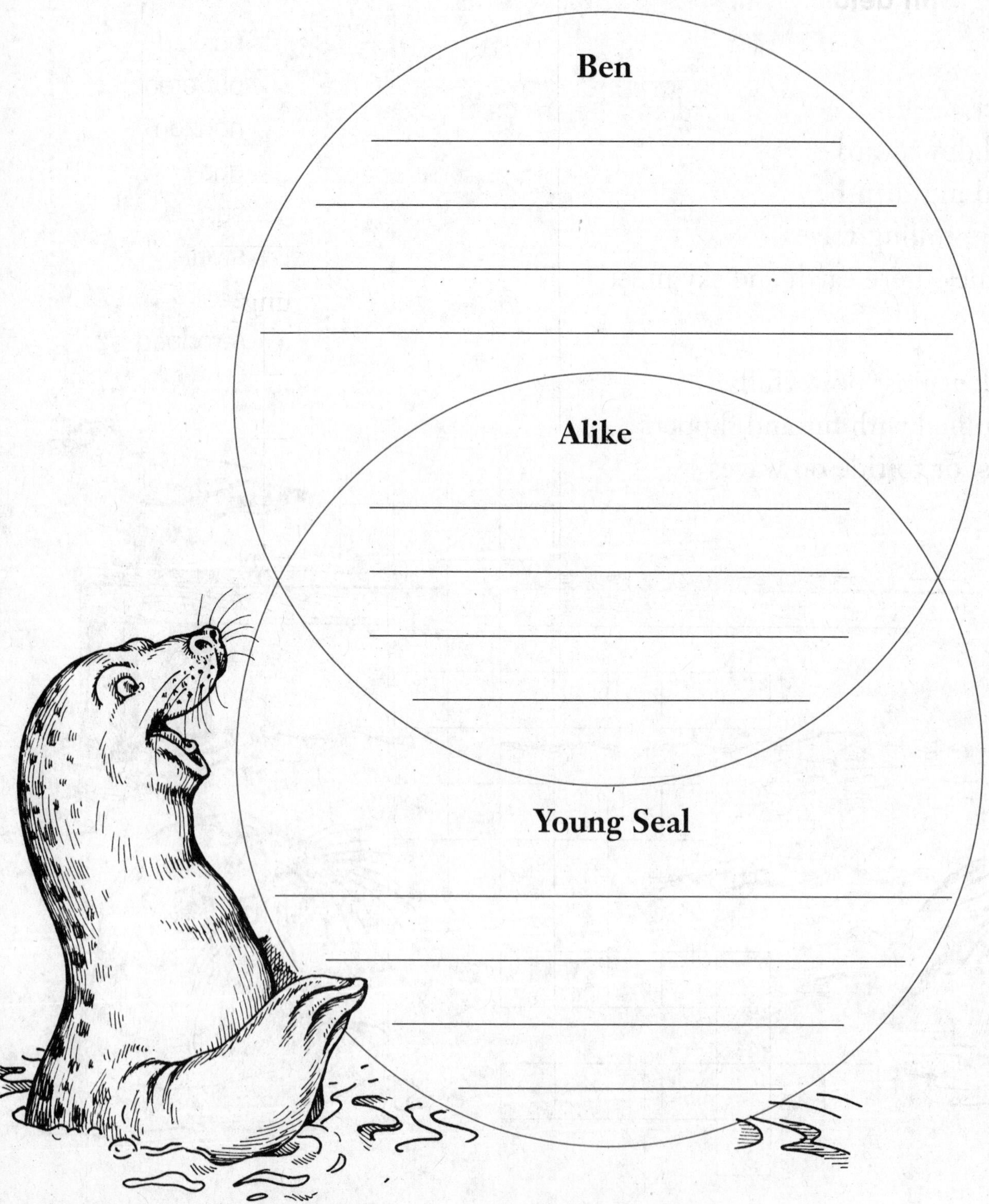

Name ______________________________

Ben's Diary

Suppose Ben kept a diary. Help him finish this page by completing the sentences with details from *Seal Surfer*.

One day when Granddad and I were on the beach, we found ______________________________.
That summer I watched as ______________________________
______________________________. All winter, my young seal friend ______________________________.

When spring came, I thought my seal friend ______________
______________. Then she returned one summer day when I was surfing. When I started to drown, she helped me by
______________________________.
I knew we would be friends forever!

Name ________________________________

Different and Alike

Read the story. Then complete the diagram on the next page.

Which Kind to Choose?

When Linda and Tracy learned they could each get a dog, the two friends found the dog books in the library. Then they started reading. Some time later, Linda said, "I'd like a dog that's friendly, loving, and loyal. Oh, and you know, my great-grandmother lives with us. She can't get out much, so we want a small dog to sit with her in the day. Also, it shouldn't need too much outdoor exercise."

Tracy said, "This book says toy poodles don't need a lot of exercise. They're also loving and like to be cuddled. And they need to be brushed every day."

"A small poodle sounds perfect for my family," Linda said. "What kind of dog is your family looking for?"

"You've seen how big our yard is," Tracy responded. "And my family loves to hike, so we're looking for a big dog that enjoys the outdoors and can keep up with us!"

"How about a Labrador retriever?" asked Linda. "It says that they love the outdoors, long walks, and exercise. They don't need as much grooming as other dogs."

"They're beautiful," Tracy said, looking at the picture. "My family would love one. But I wonder if they're friendly and loyal."

"It says they are," Linda said, looking at the book.

The girls smiled at each other and talked about dogs for hours! Which dog did each one choose? Guess!

Name ___________________________

Seal Surfer

Comprehension Skill
Compare and Contrast

Different and Alike continued

Complete the diagram with details from the story.

Toy Poodles

____

____

____

Similarities

____

____

____

Labrador Retrievers

____

____

____

Which dog would you choose — a poodle or a Labrador retriever? Why?

____

____

Seal Surfer

Structural Analysis Word Endings: *-ed, -ing*

Name ______________________________

Happy Endings

Complete the story by filling in the blanks. Build each word by adding either *-ed* or *-ing* to the word in dark type. Remember, when a base word ends with a consonant and *y*, change the *y* to *i* before adding *-ed*.

As Ellie walked beneath the maple tree, she heard a noise from above. Ellie **(look)** ________________ up and spotted a nest with two baby robins inside. The young birds **(cry)** ________________ out, "Cheep! Cheep!"

"Why are you crying?" Ellie asked the noisy birds. She **(try)** ________________ to figure out the problem. "Are you hungry?" she wondered.

"Cheep! Cheep!" the birds **(reply)** ________________.

Ellie **(start)** ________________ **(worry)** ________________ that the mother robin would not return. She hoped the mother bird was **(hurry)** ________________ back with food.

Suddenly, the mother robin appeared. She **(empty)** ________________ a beak full of worms into the mouths of her hungry babies. The young birds began **(chirp)** ________________ sweetly. It was very **(satisfy)** ________________ to see the birds so happy.

Name ____________________

Adding Endings

A **base word** is a word to which an ending may be added. When a base word ends with *e*, drop the *e* before adding *-ed* or *-ing*. When a base word ends with one vowel and one consonant, the consonant is usually doubled before *-ed* or *-ing* is added.

care – e + ed = car**ed**   grin + n + ing = gri**nning**

► In the starred word *fixing*, the *x* in *fix* is not doubled before *-ing* is added.

When a base word ends with a consonant and *y*, change the *y* to *i* before adding *-es* or *-ed*.

baby – y + ies = bab**ies**

Write each Spelling Word under the heading that shows what happens to the base word when an ending is added.

Spelling Words

1. cared
2. babies
3. chopped
4. saving
5. carried
6. fixing*
7. hurried
8. joking
9. grinning
10. smiled
11. wrapped
12. parties

Final *e* Dropped

____
____
____
____

y* Changed to *i

____
____
____
____

Final Consonant Doubled

____
____
____

No Spelling Change

____

Name ______________________________

Spelling Spree

Words in Words Write the Spelling Words that contain each of the smaller words below.

Example: top _stopped_

1. king ______________
2. rap ______________
3. are ______________
4. grin ______________
5. hop ______________
6. mile ______________

Spelling Words

1. cared
2. babies
3. chopped
4. saving
5. carried
6. fixing*
7. hurried
8. joking
9. grinning
10. smiled
11. wrapped
12. parties

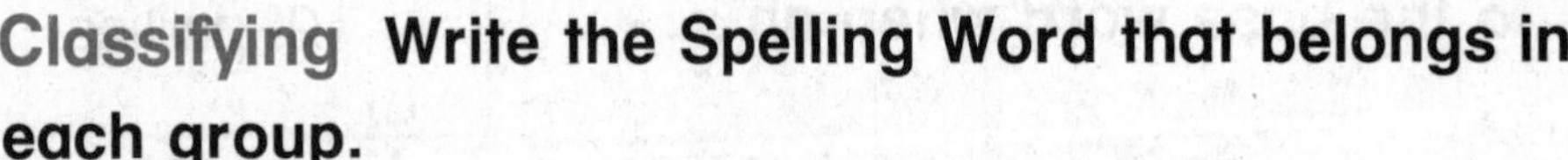

Classifying Write the Spelling Word that belongs in each group.

Example: forming, creating, _making_

7. moved, transported, ____
8. infants, toddlers, ____
9. repairing, mending, ____
10. raced, rushed, ____
11. celebrations, get-togethers, ____
12. keeping, storing, ____

7. ______________ 10. ______________

8. ______________ 11. ______________

9. ______________ 12. ______________

Name ______________________________

Proofreading and Writing

Proofreading Circle the five misspelled Spelling Words in the following journal entry. Then write each word correctly.

October 10—I fished all morning. Then I hurryed back to the harbor to meet Ben. We saw a female seal swimming in the harbor water. She looked like she was grining at us. I choped up some fish and tossed it to her. The seal ate the fish right away. Ben smiled and said, "I guess she's not interested in saveing the fish for later." The seal swam away. We wraped up the rest of our fish and brought it home. I wonder if we'll see that seal again.

Spelling Words

1. cared
2. babies
3. chopped
4. saving
5. carried
6. fixing*
7. hurried
8. joking
9. grinning
10. smiled
11. wrapped
12. parties

1. ____________________
2. ____________________
3. ____________________
4. ____________________
5. ____________________

Write About an Animal Do you have a favorite animal story? Maybe you know a funny story about a pet. Perhaps you have seen a rare or unusual animal in a zoo or aquarium. Maybe you have read a book or seen a TV program about an animal that did something remarkable.

On a separate sheet of paper, write a paragraph about an interesting animal. Use Spelling Words from the list.

Name ______________________________

Find the Right Word, the Right Meaning

Read each sentence. Then choose the correct meaning of the underlined word from the dictionary definitions below. Write the number of the correct entry and the correct meaning next to the sentence.

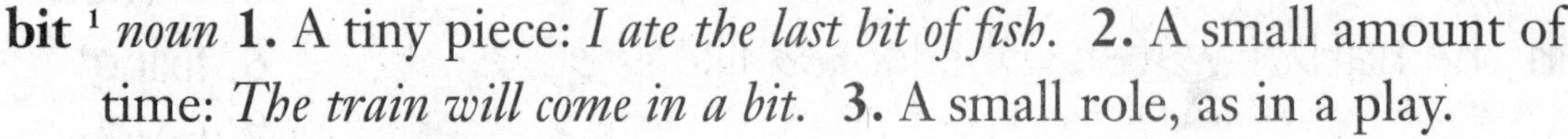

bit[1] *noun* **1.** A tiny piece: *I ate the last bit of fish.* **2.** A small amount of time: *The train will come in a bit.* **3.** A small role, as in a play.

bit[1] (bĭt) ◇ *noun, plural* **bits**

bit[2] *noun* **1.** A drilling tool. **2.** The metal mouthpiece of a bridle, used to control a horse.

bit[2] (bĭt) ◇ *noun, plural* **bits**

bit[3] *verb* Past tense and a past participle of **bite.**

bit[3] (bĭt) ◇ *verb*

1. The rider put the <u>bit</u> and the saddle on the horse.

   ____

2. I'll go to the movies with you in a <u>bit</u>.

   ____

3. The wood was so hard that it snapped the carpenter's <u>bit</u>.

   ____

4. We <u>bit</u> into the sweet apples.

   ____

5. There was just a <u>bit</u> of salad left after dinner.

   ____

Name ______________________________

Finding Helping Verbs

Circle the helping verb in each sentence. Underline the verb that it is helping.

1. Ben has watched the seals.
2. We have listened to the waves.
3. The waves have buffeted the seals.
4. The seals have arrived safely.
5. Grandfather has talked with Ben.
6. He has explained many mysteries of the sea.
7. The waves have crashed into the shore.
8. One seal has rescued Ben.
9. She has helped him.
10. You have learned about seals.

Name ______________________

Completing with Helping Verbs

Write *have* or *has* to complete each sentence.

1. We ____________ learned about seals.
2. Seals ____________ basked in the sun.
3. It ____________ warmed the seals.
4. Grandfather ____________ played Beethoven for seals.
5. They ____________ listened to the music.
6. Ben ____________ surfed with seals.
7. He ____________ watched one of the seals grow up.
8. She ____________ returned every year.
9. I ____________ enjoyed learning about seals.
10. You ____________ discovered many new facts.

Name ______________________________

Sentence Combining with Helping Verbs

Use helping verbs to combine each pair of sentences.

1. We have studied seals. We have discovered how they live.

____

2. A storm has started. A storm has threatened some seals.

____

3. The seals have dived deep. The seals have escaped.

____

4. Ben's seal has returned. Ben's seal has recognized him right away.

____

5. The waves have pushed Ben off his board. The waves have pulled him under.

____

6. A seal has pushed Ben up. A seal has saved him.

____

7. I have finished the story. I have cried at the ending.

____

8. Grandfather and Ben have watched the seals. Grandfather and Ben have admired the seals.

____

Name ______________________________

Planning a Poem

Use this graphic organizer to plan a poem of your own. Then write a poem about an experience you have had with an animal, or a place that you like very much.

Sense Words I Might Use

____

____

____

Unusual Comparisons I Might Use

____

____

____

What Is the Big Picture I Want to Create?

____

____

____

Rhythm Patterns I Might Use

____

____

____

How I Might Organize the Poem

____

____

____

Name ______________________________

Using Exact Verbs

Good writers try not to use a general verb when they can choose an exact verb to describe an action. Read these examples:

Wildflowers appeared on the rugged cliffs.
Wildflowers **bloomed** on the rugged cliffs.

The rough waves threw the seals against the rocks.
The rough waves **dashed** the seals against the rocks.

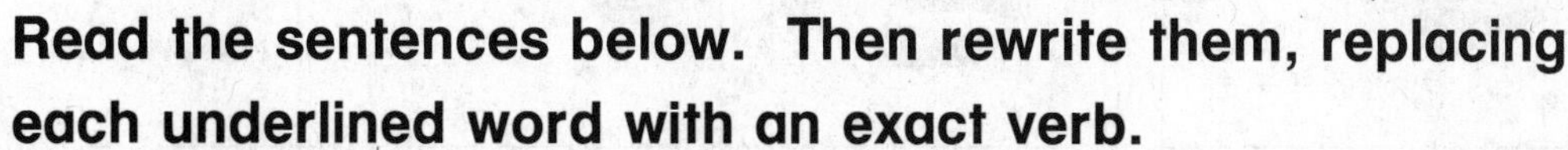

Read the sentences below. Then rewrite them, replacing each underlined word with an exact verb.

1. The face of the seal suddenly showed through the water.

____

____

2. The seal's shiny body swam in the water.

____

____

3. The boy's body dropped into the darkness of the sea.

____

____

4. The boy moved head over heels through the surf.

____

5. The seal put the boy onto his surfboard.

____

Name ______________________________

Oh, Deer!

You are a scientist observing a small group of deer. The deer are eating grass in a field near a forest of trees. Deer have never been seen in this field before. Use the Vocabulary Words to write sentences about the deer. If you need help, use your glossary.

Vocabulary

- grazing
- population
- starve
- surrounding
- territory
- wander

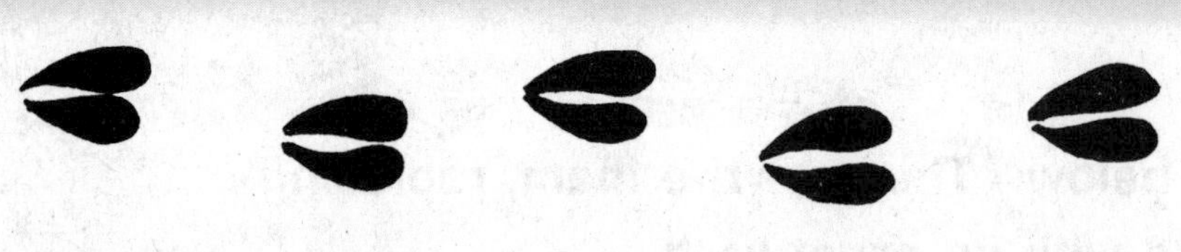

Name ______________________________

Decision Chart

Problem: ______________________________

____

____

Do you agree with how the characters solve the problem?	
***Yes,* when...**	***No,* when...**

Name ______________________________

Oh, Deer Me!

Write the following story events on the lines below in the order they occurred.

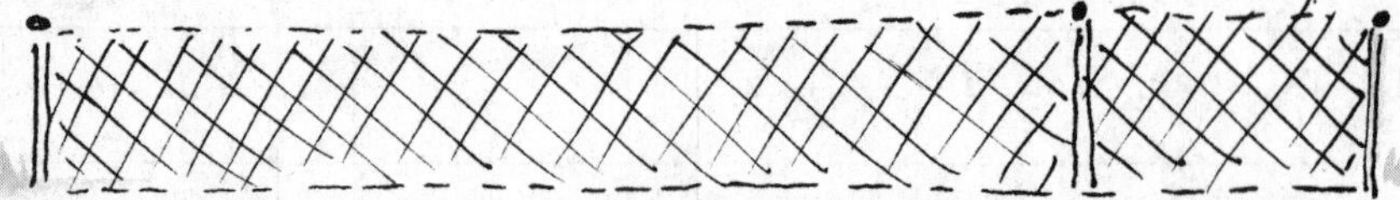

The neighbors begin a peaceful protest.
Sonia sleeps outside with the deer.
Papa calls the animal control officer.
The wildlife rescuer takes the deer away.
Deer appear in the garden.
The Pigeon Lady teaches Sonia and Peach about deer.
The neighbors order pizza.
Mr. Benny calls the wildlife rescue organization.

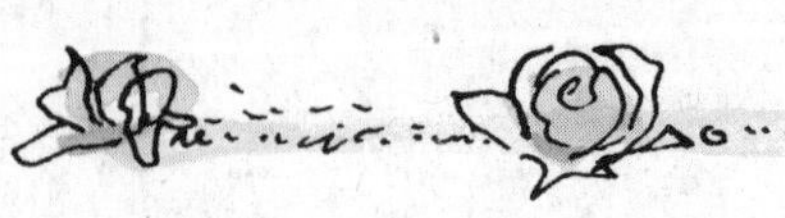

1. ______________________________

2. ______________________________

3. ______________________________

4. ______________________________

5. ______________________________

6. ______________________________

7. ______________________________

8. ______________________________

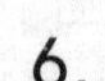

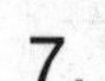

Name ___________________________

What's Best for the Neighbors?

All the neighbors must decide what to plant in the neighborhood garden. Read the dialogue. Then answer the questions on the next page.

Mrs. Rhonda: Let's grow tomatoes again. They can be canned, and we can freeze tomato sauce.

Luis: Sure, and everyone likes pizza sauce. I vote for potatoes as well. If we store them in a cool place, we can use them all winter.

Blossom: But potatoes are so cheap to buy at the store! They take too much room. I'd rather have more space for lettuce and spinach.

Mr. Yost: But I don't like spinach.

Blossom: We can plant beans and peas around the fence. That's easy enough. Then the center can be used for lettuce, spinach, and tomatoes.

Mrs. Rhonda: Shall we plant squash this year?

Luis: Squash always takes over the garden. If we plant three zucchini plants, we'll have thousands of zucchini, and we'll never use it all. It's a waste.

Mr. Yost: But zucchini bread tastes good.

Mrs. Rhonda: Here's an idea. We'll plant just one zucchini plant over here, and we can set potatoes all around it. That way, all the vines will be in the same area. Then we can plant the salad greens together and the peas and beans together too.

Name ______________________________

What's Best for the Neighbors? continued

Answer each question about the neighborhood meeting.

1. What good points does Mrs. Rhonda make in favor of planting tomatoes?

____

2. What good point does Luis make in favor of planting potatoes?

____

3. What two good points does Blossom make against growing potatoes?

____

4. Whose points are not well backed by facts?

____

5. Do you agree with Mrs. Rhonda's ideas for the garden? Why or why not?

____

____

____

Name ______________________________

What's the Word?

Prefix	Meaning	Example
un-	"not" or "the opposite of"	unable
re-	"again" or "back to"	rebuild
Suffix	**Meaning**	**Example**
-ful	"full of" or "having the qualities of"	cheerful
-er	"one who"	teacher
-ly	"in this way"	gently

Read each clue and unscramble the answer.

1. fill again: **LELRIF** ______________
2. in a kind way: **DLNKYI** ______________
3. someone who announces: **NEURNACON** ______________
4. not clear: **ACNRLEU** ______________
5. full of beauty: **LABUTUFIE** ______________
6. appear again: **PERAEPRA** ______________
7. full of help: **HPLELUF** ______________
8. someone who sings: **NIRSEG** ______________
9. the opposite of sure: **URESUN** ______________
10. in a soft way: **LYFTOS** ______________

Two Days in May

Spelling Prefixes and Suffixes (*re-, un-; -ful, -ly, -er*)

Name ______________________

Prefixes and Suffixes (*re-, un-; -ful, -ly, -er*)

A **prefix** is a word part added to the beginning of a base word. It adds meaning to the base word.

Prefix		Base Word		New Word	Meaning
re-	+	make	=	**re**make	to make again
un-	+	happy	=	**un**happy	not happy

A **suffix** is a word part added to the end of a base word. It also adds meaning to the base word.

Base Word		Suffix		New Word	Meaning
care	+	-ful	=	care**ful**	full of care
friend	+	-ly	=	friend**ly**	in a friendly way
help	+	-er	=	help**er**	one who helps

Spelling Words

1. helper
2. unfair
3. friendly
4. unhappy
5. remake
6. careful
7. hopeful
8. unlike
9. retell
10. sadly
11. farmer
12. unhurt

Write each Spelling Word under its prefix or suffix.

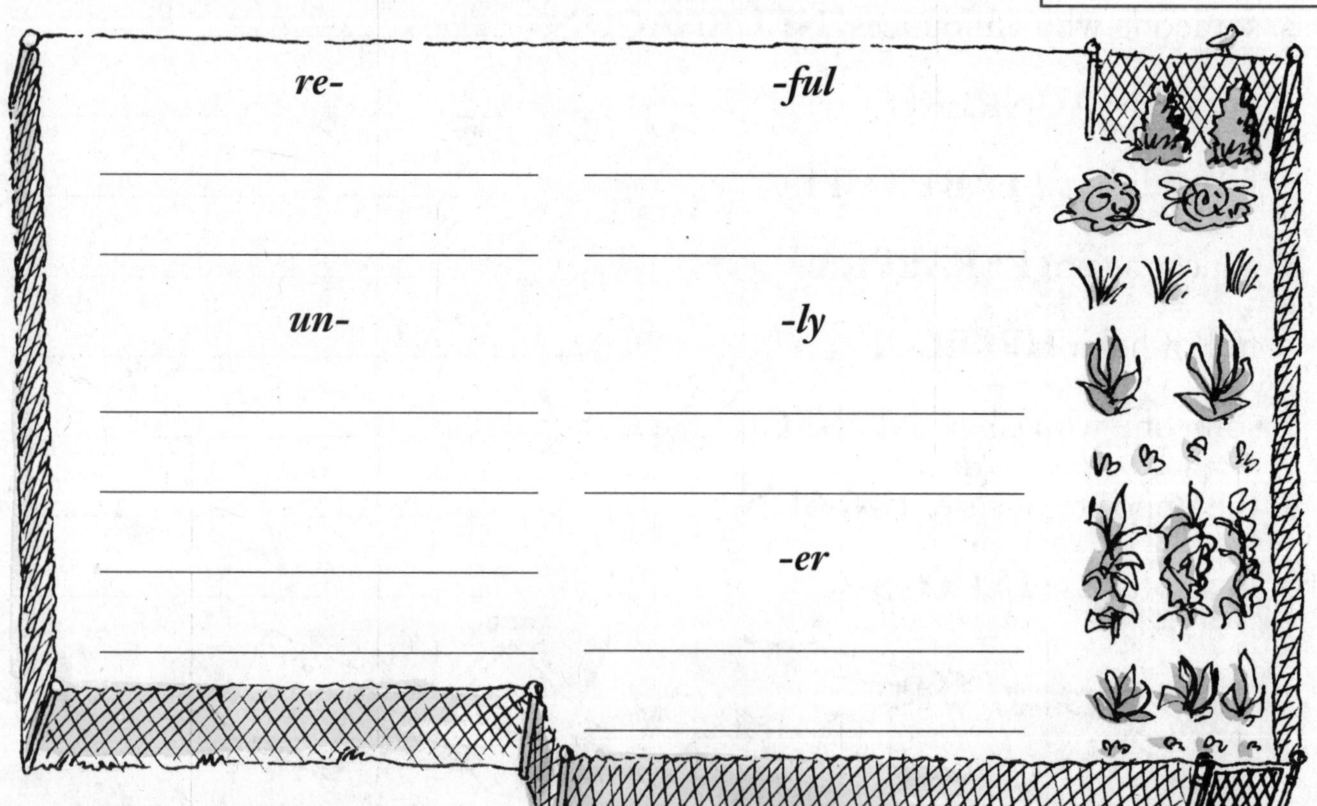

Name ______________________________

Spelling Spree

Spelling Words

1. helper
2. unfair
3. friendly
4. unhappy
5. remake
6. careful
7. hopeful
8. unlike
9. retell
10. sadly
11. farmer
12. unhurt

Base Word Hunt **Write a Spelling Word that has the same base word as each word below.**

1. friendship ______________________
2. sadness ______________________
3. helpful ______________________
4. likely ______________________
5. fairness ______________________

Prefix and Suffix Addition **Write Spelling Words by adding *re-*, *un-*, *-ful*, or *-er* to the words below.**

6. tell ______________________
7. care ______________________
8. happy ______________________
9. hope ______________________
10. make ______________________
11. hurt ______________________
12. farm ______________________

Two Days in May

Spelling Prefixes and Suffixes (*re-*, *un-*; *-ful*, *-ly*, *-er*)

Name ______________________________

Proofreading and Writing

Proofreading Circle the five misspelled Spelling Words in the report. Then write each word correctly.

Wildlife Rescue Report

Today I answered a call from a group of friendly neighbors in the city. Several deer had wandered into a backyard. The animal control officer arrived, but the people were onhappy about what he proposed to do. I came with no helpper, but I managed to get the deer onto my truck. The animals were all unhurte. A farrmer helped me herd the deer into the woods. I am hopful that they will not wander back to the city again.

Spelling Words

1. helper
2. unfair
3. friendly
4. unhappy
5. remake
6. careful
7. hopeful
8. unlike
9. retell
10. sadly
11. farmer
12. unhurt

1. ______________________
2. ______________________
3. ______________________
4. ______________________
5. ______________________

Write a Letter How would you thank Carl Jackson if you were Sonia?

On a separate sheet of paper, write a letter thanking Mr. Jackson for rescuing the deer. Tell him what you hope happens to the deer. Use Spelling Words from the list.

Name ______________________________

Two Days in May

Vocabulary Skill Dictionary: Base Words and Inflected Forms

Which Form Is It?

Read each sentence. Decide which inflected form of the base word shown in parentheses belongs in the sentence. Then write the word in the blank.

easy *adjective* Needing very little effort; not hard.
adjective **easier, easiest**

nod *verb* To move the head down and then up in a quick motion.
noun A nodding motion.
verb **nodded, nodding** *noun, plural* **nods**

rumble *verb* To make or move with a deep, long rolling sound.
noun A deep, long rolling sound.
verb **rumbled, rumbling** *noun, plural* **rumbles**

study *noun* The act or process of learning. **2.** A branch of knowledge.
verb **1.** To try to learn. **2.** To examine closely and carefully.
noun, plural **studies** *verb* **studied, studying**

1. The deer were **(nod)** ______________________________ their heads sleepily.
2. The first truck that **(rumble)** ______________________________ down the street was a delivery van.
3. Saving deer is not the **(easy)** ______________________________ task, but it's worth the effort.
4. Clarence said, "We **(study)** ______________________________ deer in science last year."
5. The wildlife rescuer **(nod)** ______________________________ in greeting.
6. Sonia felt sad as the truck was **(rumble)** ______________________________ away with the deer.

Name ___________________________________

Using Irregular Verbs

Complete each sentence with the correct form of the verb in parentheses.

1. One morning, Sonia ______________ an amazing sight. (see, past)
2. Five deer had ______________ into her yard. (come, with *had*)
3. The deer ______________ the carrot. (eat, past)
4. The neighbors ______________ to see the animals. (come, past)
5. Mr. Benny has ______________ deer in the wild. (see, with *has*)
6. By morning, the deer had ______________ a lot of flowers. (eat, with *had*)
7. We have ______________ everything we can. (did, with *have*)
8. The wildlife rescuer ______________ to catch the deer. (go, past)
9. He ______________ his job very well. (do, past)
10. The van with the deer has ______________ to the country. (go, with *has*)

Name ______________________________

Completing Sentences with Irregular Verbs

Complete each sentence with the correct form of the verb in parentheses.

1. The wildlife rescuer ____________________ the deer medicine to make it tired. (give, past)

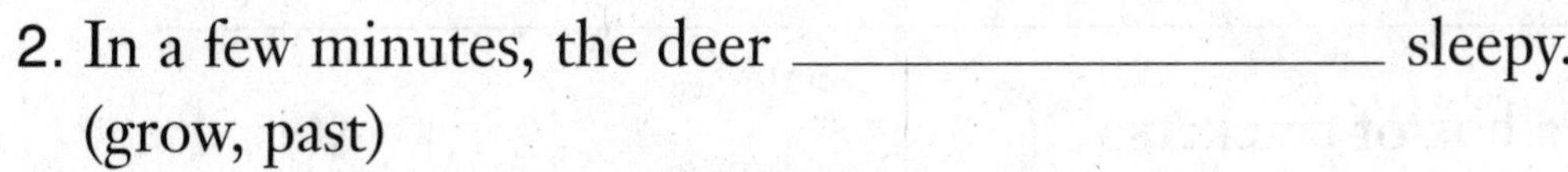

2. In a few minutes, the deer ____________________ sleepy. (grow, past)
3. The man ____________________ the deer away from the city. (take, past)
4. The neighbors had ____________________ many photographs of the deer. (took, with *had*).
5. The deer have ____________________ happily in their new home. (run, with *have*)
6. The young deer have ____________________ a lot since they were born. (grow, with *have*)
7. A reporter ____________________ about the deer in Sonia's yard. (write, past)
8. He has ____________________ the story to his editor. (give, with *has*)
9. Sonia ____________________ to show the article to her friends. (run, past)
10. She has ____________________ a poem about the deer. (write, with *has*)

Name ____

Using the Correct Verb Form

Read each sentence. If the verb is correct, write C after the sentence. If the verb is incorrect, rewrite the sentence with the correct form.

1. A squirrel comed into Sonia's house.

____

2. It has eated a box of crackers.

____

3. Sonia runned to tell her parents about the squirrel.

____

4. They saw the cracker crumbs in the kitchen.

____

5. The squirrel had ran out the window.

____

6. They wented to the yard.

____

7. The squirrel went up a tree.

____

8. Sonia has seed the squirrel again.

____

Name ______________________________

Problem-Solution Planner

Use this page to help you plan a problem-solution essay. Work with a partner. Think of a problem and two ideas to solve it. Tell what happened with each idea. End with a sentence or two that tells how the problem was solved.

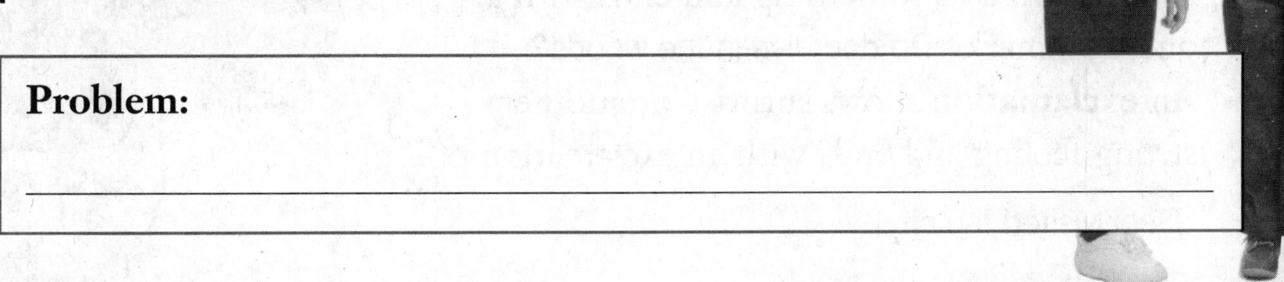

Problem:

____

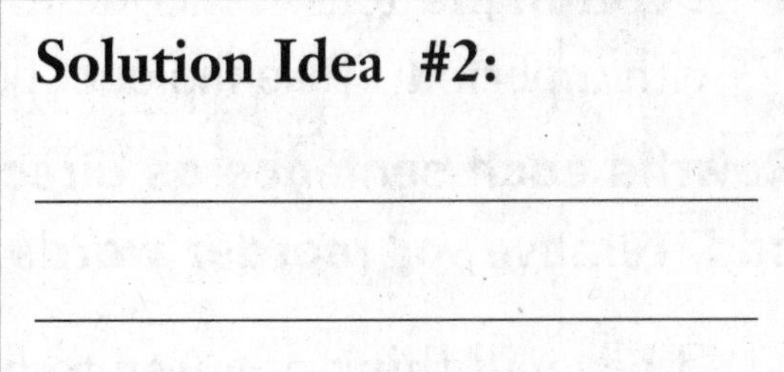

Solution Idea #1:

____

____

What happened:

____

____

____

Solution Idea #2:

____

____

What happened:

____

____

____

Problem Solved!

____

____

Name ______________________________

Varying Sentence Types

Writers use the four kinds of sentences to make their writing more interesting.

- A **statement** tells something and ends with a period: Deer live in the woods.
- A **question** asks something and ends with a question mark: Do deer live in the woods?
- An **exclamation** shows surprise or another strong feeling and ends with an exclamation point: Deer visited the city!
- A **command** tells someone to do something and ends with a period: Take the deer back to the woods.

Rewrite each sentence as directed. You may need to add, remove, or reorder words to change sentence types.

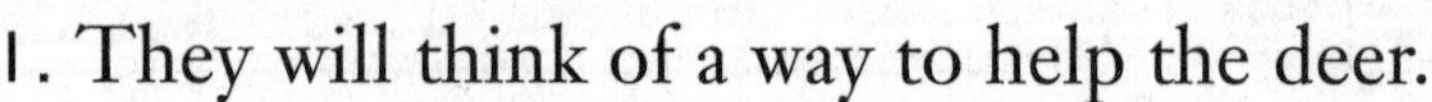

1. They will think of a way to help the deer.

   Command: ______________________________

2. Are wild animals safe in the city?

   Exclamation: ______________________________

3. Call the animal control officers.

   Statement: ______________________________

4. What do you see out the window?

   Command: ______________________________

5. There are four deer in the garden.

   Question: ______________________________

Name ______________________________

Sharing Words

Write the correct Key Vocabulary word to complete each sentence. Then answer the question that follows.

Vocabulary

cherished
companion
drudgery
dwellers
furrows
refresh
shunned

1. The mice lived in the cornfield. They were field ________________.
2. To ________________ themselves, the mice sipped raindrops.
3. The mice liked to hide in the narrow ________________ between the rows of corn.
4. For the tiny mice, gathering corn every day was ________________.
5. The mice ________________ the barn, because a dangerous cat lived there.
6. One mouse was lonely, and wanted a ________________.
7. He became friends with a bird, and they ________________ the time they spent together.
8. What is a person, place, or thing you cherish?

____

____

Monitoring Student Progress

Graphic Organizer Compare and Contrast

Name ______________________________

Compare and Contrast Animals

Use the chart below to list three animals from each selection. Then write a few words about what each animal does.

Story	Animals	What they do
Alejandro's Gift	1. ________ 2. ________ 3. ________	________ ________ ________
The Living Desert	1. ________ 2. ________ 3. ________	________ ________ ________ ________ ________ ________

What do the animals in these stories have in common? How are they different?

____

____

____

Monitoring Student Progress

Connecting and Comparing
Making Judgments

Name ___________________________

Giving and Receiving

Compare the people and animals in *Alejandro's Gift* and *Two Days in May*. Complete the chart below and then answer the question that follows.

	Alejandro's Gift	*Two Days in May*
Setting		
Main characters		
How the animals and people meet		
What the people do for the animals		
What the animals do for the people		

In these stories, do you think animals help the people more, or do you think people help the animals more? Why?

____

____

____

Monitoring Student Progress

Key Vocabulary The Living Desert

Name ______________________________

Life in the Desert

Fill in each blank with the correct word from the list.

Vocabulary

saguaro
environment
moisture
tenants
behavior
cope

1. The opposite of *dryness* is ________________.
2. An animal's ________________ is the way the animal acts.
3. The desert is one type of ________________.
4. Desert animals must ________________ with having little water.
5. A ________________ is a kind of cactus.
6. The people or animals who live in a place are called ________________.
7. Choose two or more Key Vocabulary words and use them to write a sentence or two about life in the desert.

____

____

Name ______________________________

Test Practice

Use the three steps you've learned to choose the best answer for these vocabulary questions about *The Living Desert*. Fill in the circle next to the best answer.

1. Read this sentence from the story. "Think of the saguaro cactus as an apartment building and restaurant, an environment that feeds and houses many desert creatures." What does *houses* mean?

   ○ threatens ○ pricks
   ○ harms ○ protects

2. Which word means about the same as *nectar* on page 114?

   ○ juice ○ color
   ○ dust ○ heat

3. The author writes, "The woodpeckers make new nests each year, and the empty holes gain new tenants." Which word means the opposite of *empty*?

   ○ shallow ○ full
   ○ dark ○ brown

4. On page 114, what does the word *handy* mean?

   ○ hard to find
   ○ very useful
   ○ difficult to see
   ○ not soft

Continue on page 58.

Name ______________________________

Test Practice continued

5. In paragraph 1 on page 116, what does the word *surface* mean?

   ◯ the roughest part
   ◯ something that is round
   ◯ the outside layer
   ◯ a smooth edge

6. Which word means about the same as *den* on page 116?

   ◯ air
   ◯ tree
   ◯ nest
   ◯ rock

7. Read this sentence from the story: "Finally there are those creatures that actually seek the sun." What does *seek* mean?

   ◯ sleep inside of
   ◯ hide behind
   ◯ run away from
   ◯ look for

8. Read this sentence from the story: "Lizards need to bask in the heat to warm up their bodies enough to become active." What does the word *bask* mean?

   ◯ to eat a meal
   ◯ to sniff the air
   ◯ to lie around
   ◯ to hunt at night

Monitoring Student Progress

Comprehension Skill Fact and Opinion

Name ______________________________

Can You Prove It?

Read each sentence. Write *F* if the sentence is a fact. Write *O* if the sentence is an opinion.

1. Seals give birth to their pups on land. _____
2. Most newborn pups are covered with a fine, soft fur. _____
3. Harbor seals are my favorite type of seal. _____
4. Seals live both on land and in the water. _____
5. Watching seals underwater is better than watching them on land. _____
6. It is fun to watch seals swim. _____
7. Killer whales, sharks, and polar bears are a seal's main natural enemies. _____
8. It is sad when a seal gets caught in an oil spill. _____
9. Walruses are the strangest looking animals in the sea. _____
10. Fish and squid are the primary food of fur seals. _____

Name ______________________________

Was It a Good Decision?

Read the paragraph. Then fill in the chart below to record your ideas about the decision made by the characters.

Stuart and Teresa were walking to school. As they came around the corner, Stuart noticed something strange ahead of them. A bird's nest was lying on a pile of leaves below a tree. When the two friends got closer, they saw three spotted eggs in it. Teresa looked up in the tree and saw a large low branch.

"The nest must have been blown from that big branch," she said.

"Let's take these eggs to Ms. Jepson, the fourth-grade teacher," said Stuart. "She knows a lot about birds."

Teresa gently lifted the nest and wrapped it in a napkin. Then, cradling the package carefully, she followed Stuart on the path toward school.

Solution: Take the nest and eggs to Ms. Jepson at school.	
Pros	**Cons**
Is this the right decision? Why or why not?	

Monitoring Student Progress

Structural Analysis More Prefixes and Suffixes

Name ______________________________

Mix and Match Words

Read the prefixes, suffixes, and base words. Then read each sentence. Combine a prefix or suffix with a base word to form a word that completes the sentence. Write the word on the line. (The base words can be used more than once.)

Prefixes	Base Words	Suffixes
un- "not"	kind play sure	*-ly* "in a certain way"
re- "again"	quick wind	*-ful* "full of"
pre- "before"	help cook	*-er* "someone who"

1. My brother likes to ______________ videos of his soccer games.
2. The deer were ______________ which way they should turn.
3. We had to run ______________ to catch the school bus.
4. Dad said he'll ______________ our dinners before we go camping.
5. Tina tried to be ______________ when her neighbor broke his arm.
6. The nurse smiled at me ______________.
7. You are the best ______________ on our soccer team.
8. Please ______________ the video after you watch it.
9. It is ______________ to tease people.
10. I need a ______________ to clean up this mess.

Name ______________________________

Find the Right Definition

Read the entries for each multiple-meaning word. Then read each sentence. Write on the line the number of the definition that makes sense in the sentence.

batter (*verb*) **1.** To hit repeatedly with heavy blows.
batter (*noun*) **2.** The player at bat in baseball.
batter (*noun*) **3.** A beaten mixture used in cooking.

1. The batter hit a home run. _____
2. We poured the cake batter into the pan. _____
3. She watched the waves batter her boat. _____

duck (*noun*) **1.** A water bird with a flat bill and webbed feet.
duck (*verb*) **2.** To lower the head or body quickly.
duck (*noun*) **3.** A closely woven cotton fabric.

1. The jacket was made of blue duck. _____
2. The duck paddled behind the boat. _____
3. He had to duck, or the ball would have hit him. _____

Name ______________________________

Spelling Review

Write Spelling Words from the list on this page to answer the questions.

1–8. Which eight words have the vowel + *r* sound in *hair*?

1. ____________ 5. ____________

2. ____________ 6. ____________

3. ____________ 7. ____________

4. ____________ 8. ____________

9–16. Which eight words have endings that have changed the spelling of the base word?

9. ____________ 13. ____________

10. ____________ 14. ____________

11. ____________ 15. ____________

12. ____________ 16. ____________

17–21. Which five words have the prefix *re-* or *un-*?

17. ____________ 20. ____________

18. ____________ 21. ____________

19. ____________

22–25. Which four words have the suffix *-ful*, *-ly*, or *-er*?

22. ____________ 24. ____________

23. ____________ 25. ____________

Spelling Words

1. sadly
2. helper
3. unhurt
4. parties
5. pear
6. retell
7. chair
8. joking
9. unlike
10. scare
11. pair
12. cared
13. babies
14. hopeful
15. air
16. grinning
17. bare
18. chopped
19. care
20. carried
21. friendly
22. bear
23. unhappy
24. remake
25. smiled

Name ______________________________

Spelling Spree

Wacky Rhymes Write a Spelling Word in each sentence that rhymes with the underlined word.

Spelling Words

1. air
2. parties
3. grinning
4. pear
5. chair
6. carried
7. babies
8. chopped
9. pair
10. joking
11. unhappy
12. retell

1. I will wear a ______________ of new socks to the fair.
2. Who got hair on my good ______________?
3. She's ______________ because our team is winning.
4. They are ______________ and poking at piñatas.
5. When my parents got married, my mother ______________ roses.

Riddle Time Write a Spelling Word to answer each question.

6. What do you blow into a balloon? ______________
7. What is a yellow or green fruit that grows on trees? ______________
8. What do you do if you recite a story again? ______________
9. How does somebody wearing a frown feel? ______________
10. What has been done to a cut-up apple? ______________
11. Who are the youngest people? ______________
12. What events can you go to on birthdays? ______________

Name ______________________________

Proofreading and Writing

Proofreading **Circle the six misspelled Spelling Words in this story. Then write each word correctly.**

Marv, the farm helpir, worked hard and caired for some baby rabbits that were unliek others because they were very small. He would reemake their beds in his freindly way. Marv was hopefull they would grow stronger soon.

1. ______________ 4. ______________

2. ______________ 5. ______________

3. ______________ 6. ______________

Spelling Words

1. care
2. friendly
3. smiled
4. unlike
5. sadly
6. scare
7. bare
8. grinning
9. helper
10. cared
11. remake
12. bear
13. hopeful
14. unhurt

Tale of a Bear **Use Spelling Words to complete this story beginning.**

Mimi watched the polar 7. ______________ cub. His 8. ______________ head made her shiver. Mimi looked at the cub 9. ______________. Mimi's dad knew that she wanted to take 10. ______________ of the cub. He told her it was 11. ______________ by the cold, and icebergs didn't 12. ______________ it. Then Mimi 13. ______________ happily. She even started 14. ______________.

Write a Description **On a separate sheet of paper, write about your favorite animal and where it lives. Use the Spelling Review Words.**

Name ______________________

Choosing Forms of *be*

Choose the correct verb to complete each sentence. Write it in the blank.

1. The desert ______________ dry most of the year. (is, are)
2. Many desert plants ______________ small. (is, are)
3. Last month ______________ rainy. (was, were)
4. The desert animals ______________ busy. (was, were)
5. I ______________ a good hiker, and so is my dad. (am, is)
6. We ______________ ready for a long hike last week. (was, were)
7. The desert trail ______________ wet in places. (was, were)
8. You ______________ probably a good hiker. (am, are)
9. February ______________ a fine month for a desert hike. (is, are)
10. You ______________ a good observer. (was, were)

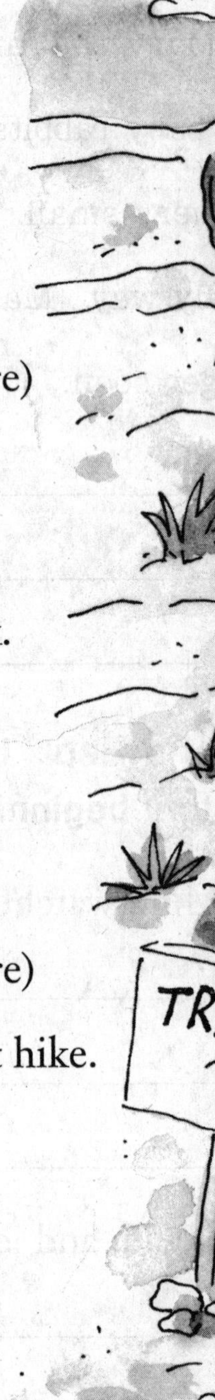

Name ______________________________

Writing Irregular Verbs

Complete each sentence with the correct form of the verb in parentheses.

1. My cousin ______________ to the desert last month. (*go*, past)
2. She had ______________ to the desert once before. (*go*, with *had*)
3. She ______________ a camera with her. (*take*, past)
4. By noon she had ______________ twenty pictures. (*take*, with *had*)
5. A ranger ______________ a talk about desert animals. (*give*, past)
6. He had ______________ a desert fox a week before. (*see*, with *had*)
7. My cousin ______________ notes about the animals. (*write*, past)
8. She has ______________ me a letter about her trip. (*write*, with *has*)
9. She ______________ a good job. (*do*, past)
10. She has ______________ me a lot of information about life in the desert. (*give*, with *has*)

Name ________________________________

Biography Words

Rearrange the words in each box to write a definition for each numbered word.

story person's life a

1. biography: ________________________________

are things true that

2. facts: ________________________________

following one another after thing

3. sequence: ________________________________

that happen things

4. events: ________________________________

subject a study careful of

5. research: ________________________________

Answer each question. Write Yes or No.

6. Can facts be made up? ____________
7. Is a novel a kind of biography? ____________
8. Are baseball games and air shows events? ____________
9. Are the dates 1910, 1863, 2004, and 1945 in sequence? ____________
10. Is reading about a person and taking notes called research?

____

Name ______________________

Facts and Conclusions

Facts About ______________________

1.
2.
3.
4.
5.
6.

Conclusions About ______________________

1. ______________________

____

2. ______________________

____

Name ______________________

Best Beginnings

Write a shorter version of the opening sentences of each biography. Then describe which opening most made you want to read the rest of the biography.

Becoming a Champion: The Babe Didrikson Story

____

____

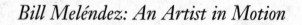

Bill Meléndez: An Artist in Motion

____

____

Brave Bessie Coleman: Pioneer Aviator

____

____

Hank Greenberg: All-Around All-Star

____

____

Which opening made you want to read the biography?

____

How might reading this biography change your life?

____

____

Name ______________________________

When They Were Young

Write one fact about each person's childhood. Tell how that fact affected each person as an adult.

Babe Didrikson

____

____

Bill Meléndez

____

____

Bessie Coleman

____

____

Hank Greenberg

____

____

What is something you can do as a young person that will help you when you are grown up?

____

____

Name ______________________________

Reading a Biography

Facts About ______________________________

1.
2.
3.
4.
5.
6.

Conclusions About ______________________________

1. ______________________________

____

2. ______________________________

____

Name ______________________________

Suffix It!

Some suffixes can change a base word from one part of speech to another. For example, adding *-er* to the verb *train* turns it into the noun *trainer.* Adding *-ful* to the noun *wonder* changes it to the adjective *wonderful.*

Fill in the blanks below by adding *-y, -ly, -ful, -er, -less,* or *-ness* to each word in dark type so it fits the sentence.

I saw a small brown caterpillar **(slow)** ______________ crawling up a tree. Its coat looked so soft and **(fuzz)** ______________ that I had to touch it. I was **(care)** ______________ and tried not to disturb it. But it started moving more **(quick)** ______________ as soon as I reached toward it. I felt sorry for disturbing the **(help)** ______________ little creature. The next day, I walked by the tree again. There was no sign of the caterpillar. I felt **(hope)** ______________ about ever seeing it again. But a few weeks later, I noticed a beautiful butterfly in the tree. I was filled with **(glad)** ______________! I wish I were a **(paint)** ______________ so I could capture its beautiful colors. My small brown caterpillar turned into a real beauty!

Name ______________________

Changing Final *y* to *i*

When a base word ends with a consonant and *y*, change the *y* to *i* before adding *-ed*, *-es*, *-er*, or *-est*.

puppy − y + ies = pupp**ies** happy − y + ier = happ**ier**
cry − y + ied = cr**ied** dry − y + iest = dri**est**

Spelling Words

1. puppies
2. flies
3. stories
4. skies
5. driest
6. candies
7. pennies
8. cried
9. ponies
10. bunnies
11. happier
12. funniest

Write each Spelling Word under its ending.

-es

____
____
____
____
____
____
____
____

-ed

____

-er

____

-est

____
____

Name ______________________________

Spelling Spree

Word Clues One Spelling Word is the plural of a word that has the same meaning as the underlined clue. Write the Spelling Word.

1. Not one small horse but many ______________
2. Not one rabbit but many ______________
3. Not one tale in a book but many ______________
4. Not one baby dog but many ______________
5. Not one sugary treat but many ______________
6. Not one buzzing insect but many ______________
7. Not one cent but many ______________

Spelling Words

1. puppies
2. flies
3. stories
4. skies
5. driest
6. candies
7. pennies
8. cried
9. ponies
10. bunnies
11. happier
12. funniest

Comparing Write the Spelling Word that completes each sentence.

8. The clown with the red nose is the ______________ of the three clowns.
9. I feel ______________ when it is sunny than when it is raining.
10. July was the ______________ month last year.

Name ______________________________

Proofreading and Writing

Proofreading Circle the five misspelled Spelling Words in this part of a biography. Then write each word correctly.

Alfred Flyte loved to fly in his hot-air balloon. He thought other people might like to ride in it, too. He took his balloon all around the country. Because he was a rich man, he gave rides at very low prices.

"Take a balloon ride for just penneys!" he cryed. "Come join me in the skyies!"

Alfred was never happeir than when he was flying. As Alfred got older, he stopped flying, but he never stopped telling amazing storyes about his days as a balloon pilot.

1. ______________
2. ______________
3. ______________
4. ______________
5. ______________

Spelling Words

1. puppies
2. flies
3. stories
4. skies
5. driest
6. candies
7. pennies
8. cried
9. ponies
10. bunnies
11. happier
12. funniest

Write an Introduction Suppose that someone you know is going to speak to an audience. You have been asked to introduce the speaker. What important facts would you tell about that person?

On a separate piece of paper, write an introduction about the person. Use Spelling Words from the list.

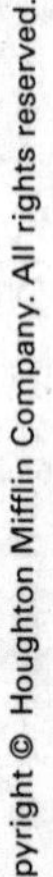

Name ______________________________

Jargon Jane

Jane is great at every sport she plays, as you will soon see. Read the paragraph below and fill in the blanks with words from the box. Use the right jargon for each sport Jane plays.

dribbles	goal	hole in one	home run
pop-up fly	serves	slam dunk	volley

What is Jane's best sport? That's hard to say. When she plays baseball, she always hits at least one ______________. Out on the field, she catches every ______________ that comes her way. During soccer season, Jane always scores the winning ______________. When it's time for basketball, Jane is the one who ______________ the ball down the court and scores the big points. Because she's so tall, she can reach up and ______________ the ball into the hoop. But that's not all. She golfs too! When she hits that little white ball, you know she's going to get a ______________. Did I mention her tennis game? She ______________ that tennis ball so fast, you don't even see it coming. She can ______________ with you for hours, hitting the ball back and forth tirelessly. But she also can beat you in no time flat. That's why I prefer to watch Jane from the sidelines.

Name ______________________________

Simple and Compound Sentences

Combine each pair of simple sentences into a compound sentence, using a comma and the joining word *and* or *but*.

1. Bessie Coleman learned to fly in France. No one would hire her in the United States.

____

____

2. An air show took place in 1922. Bessie was a pilot in it.

____

____

3. Bessie wanted to start an aviation school. She was killed in a plane crash.

____

____

Separate each compound sentence into two simple sentences. Use correct capitalization and punctuation.

4. Walt Disney studios hired Bill Meléndez, and he worked as an animator there.

____

____

5. Many animators use computers now, but in 1938 Meléndez drew everything by hand.

____

____

Name ______________________________

Varied Sentences

Rewrite this paragraph so that it has both simple and compound sentences. Create three compound sentences. Remember to use correct punctuation and joining words.

Satchel Paige was a great pitcher. Blacks were not allowed in the major leagues in the 1920s. Paige played for twenty years in the Negro Leagues. In 1947 the Brooklyn Dodgers finally hired a black player, Jackie Robinson. The Dodgers broke the barrier. Other teams followed. The Cleveland Indians heard about Paige. They asked him to join their team. He played for them until 1949. In 1971 Satchel Paige was elected to the National Baseball Hall of Fame.

____

____

____

____

____

____

____

____

Name ______________________________

Using Verbs Correctly

Use proofreading marks to correct the ten errors in capitalization, end punctuation, and verb forms in this paragraph about the pilot Amelia Earhart.

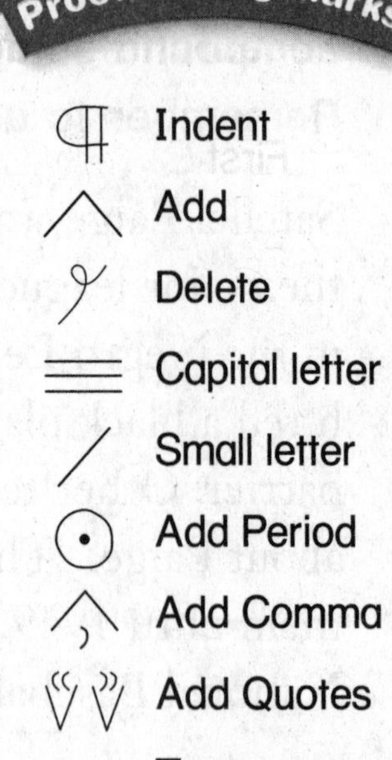

Proofreading Marks
Indent
Add
Delete
Capital letter
Small letter
Add Period
Add Comma
Add Quotes
Transpose

Example: airplane travel ~~growed~~ grew more and more popular in the 1920s.

Amelia Earhart were a famous pilot. she was the first woman to fly alone across the Atlantic Ocean. She writed a book about her experience. In 1935 she goed to Hawaii to fly alone from there to California, another first. In 1937 Amelia earhart and Fred Noonan tryed to fly around the world. They disappeared in the middle of the Pacific oceans. No one ever found Amelia's plane The mystery may never be solved?

Name ______________________________

Writing a Biography

I will write about ________________.

Researching Facts

First Source ________________	Second Source ________________
Facts	Facts

Name ______________________________

Beginnings for Biographies

A good opening sentence does two things. It states the topic and catches the reader's attention.

Make a check mark by the stronger of each pair of opening sentences. Then tell why it is better.

1. ___ This biography is about a great man.

   ___ Abraham Lincoln led our country during very difficult times.

Reason: ______________________________

____

2. ___ When Sarah Hughes glides over the ice, it's clear that she has worked hard for her goals.

   ___ Sarah Hughes is good at what she does.

Reason: ______________________________

____

3. ___ Now I'm going to write about someone who could play the piano.

   ___ Mozart made playing the piano look easy.

Reason: ______________________________

____

____

Name ____________________

Voyagers

If you were to take a voyage, where would you go? Describe the place and tell why you would go there.

Would you go alone or with other people? What things would you bring with you?

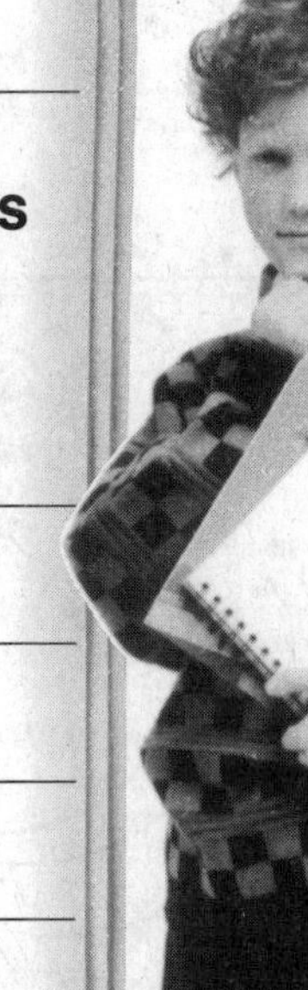

Name ______________________________

Voyagers

Fill in the chart as you read the stories.

	Across the Wide Dark Sea	Yunmi and Halmoni's Trip	Trapped by the Ice!
Who takes the voyage? Where does the voyage begin and end?			
What qualities help the voyagers succeed?			

Name ______________________

Tale of a Sea Voyage

On the line after each sentence, write the correct definition of the underlined word.

Definitions You Will Need:

- heavy metal object that keeps a ship in place
- crowded
- trip from one place to another
- passing slowly through small openings
- small community in a new place
- stay alive
- tired

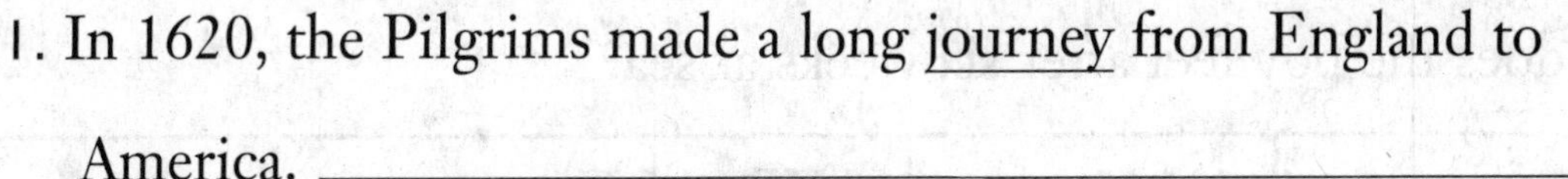

1. In 1620, the Pilgrims made a long <u>journey</u> from England to America. ______________________
2. With so many people, the ship was <u>cramped</u>. ______________________
3. Water kept <u>seeping</u> through the wooden walls of the ship. ______________________
4. When the ship neared land, the crew dropped the <u>anchor</u>. ______________________
5. The many hardships made the Pilgrims <u>weary</u>. ______________________
6. Even though the voyage was very difficult, all but one of the passengers managed to <u>survive</u>. ______________________
7. After the Pilgrims landed, they chose a spot and built a <u>settlement</u>. ______________________

Name ___________________________

Inference Chart

1. How does the boy feel when the journey begins?	
Story Clues (pages 158–161) He looks ahead at the wide dark sea. ___________ ___________	**What I Know** ___________ ___________ ___________
My Inference ___________	

2. How does the boy feel after six weeks at sea?	
Story Clues (pages 162–165) ___________ ___________	**What I Know** ___________ ___________
My Inference ___________	

3. How do the people react to the report of the new land?	
Story Clues (pages 168–170) ___________ ___________	**What I Know** ___________ ___________
My Inference ___________	

Name ______________________________

Report on the Journey

Use a complete sentence to answer each question about *Across the Wide Dark Sea*.

1. What are some things the Pilgrims bring with them on the *Mayflower*? ______________________________

____

2. Why does the boy tire of being on the ship week after week? ______________________________

____

3. What serious damage does one storm do to the *Mayflower*? ______________________________

____

4. Why do the people on the *Mayflower* make the dangerous journey?

____

5. What do the people fear when they want to go ashore? ______________________________

____

6. Where do the Pilgrims decide to start their new settlement?

____

7. What are some of the things the Indians teach the Pilgrims? ______________________________

____

8. How do the boy and his father feel about the new settlement in the spring? ______________________________

Name ______________________________

Making Good Guesses

Read the story. Then answer the questions on the next page.

A Trip Back in Time!

When Dad said we were going to Plymouth to see where the Pilgrims lived, Mom looked at us sharply. She said, "I want you two to behave and learn something today." My sister Margie smiled and winked at me when Mom looked away.

The place was not at all what we expected. Instead of a museum display, we found ourselves walking past full-sized homes with fences and gardens. It looked like New Plymouth might have looked in 1627. People who dressed and talked like Pilgrims answered our questions as they went about their tasks for the day. It seemed as if we had been carried back in time.

The best part of our visit happened by chance. We were looking at the goats when a young Pilgrim girl came by with a bucket of water. She told us how the brown goat had kicked her last week. Then she invited us into her home, which turned out to be a small, cramped, hot, smoky cottage with a cooking fire right on the dirt floor. It was as if we'd made a new friend. We learned all about Mary, how she did chores most of the day, how she hated to milk goats, how she loved to shine the kettle with salt and vinegar. And she was so polite to all the adults! Why, she even curtsied to my parents. Needless to say, we were too busy talking to get into trouble — well, on that day anyway!

Name ______________________________

Making Good Guesses continued

Use clues from the story and what you know to answer each question.

1. What was Margie planning to do?

____

Story Clues	What I Know
____________________	____________________
____________________	____________________

2. How does the storyteller feel about the Pilgrim girl's home?

____

Story Clues	What I Know
____________________	____________________
____________________	____________________

3. What does the storyteller realize about the life of a Pilgrim girl?

____

Story Clues	What I Know
____________________	____________________
____________________	____________________
____________________	____________________

Name ____________________

Riddled with Suffixes

Each word below contains a base word and a suffix. Write each base word. Put only one letter on each line. To solve the riddle, write each numbered letter on the line with the matching number below.

1. darkness ___ ___ ___ ___ (4)
2. kindness ___ ___ ___ ___ (9)
3. sunless ___ ___ ___ (7)
4. careless ___ ___ ___ ___ (5)
5. hopeless ___ ___ ___ ___ (6, 3)
6. worthless ___ ___ ___ ___ ___ (1)
7. goodness ___ ___ ___ ___ (2)
8. emptiness ___ ___ ___ ___ ___
9. priceless ___ ___ ___ ___ ___ (8)
10. fearless ___ ___ ___ ___

Native Americans shared more than their food with the settlers. They also shared their language. Solve the puzzle to learn one Native American word we use in English.

___ ___ ___ ___ ___ ___ ___ ___ ___
1 2 3 4 5 6 7 8 9

Name ____________________

The Vowel Sounds in *tooth* and *cook*

When you hear the /o͞o/ sound, as in *tooth* or *chew*, remember that it may be spelled with the pattern *oo* or *ew*. The /o͝o/ sound, as in *cook*, may be spelled with the pattern *oo*.

/o͞o/ tooth, chew

/o͝o/ cook

► In the starred words *shoe* and *blue*, the /o͞o/ sound is spelled *oe* or *ue*.

Write each Spelling Word under its vowel sound.

Spelling Words

1. tooth
2. chew
3. grew
4. cook
5. shoe*
6. blue*
7. boot
8. flew
9. shook
10. balloon
11. drew
12. spoon

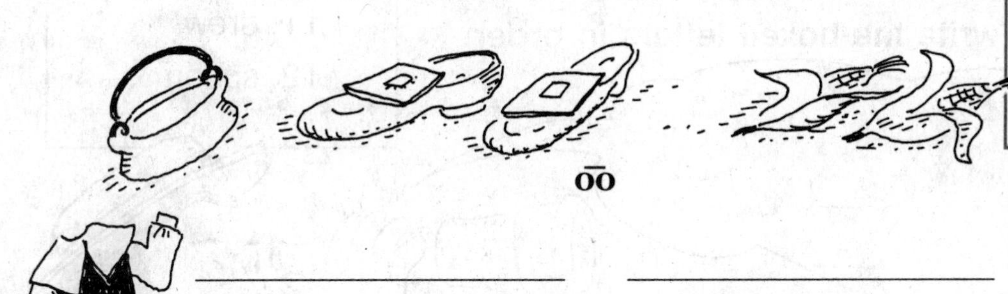

o͞o

________ ________

________ ________

________ ________

________ ________

________ ________

o͝o

________ ________

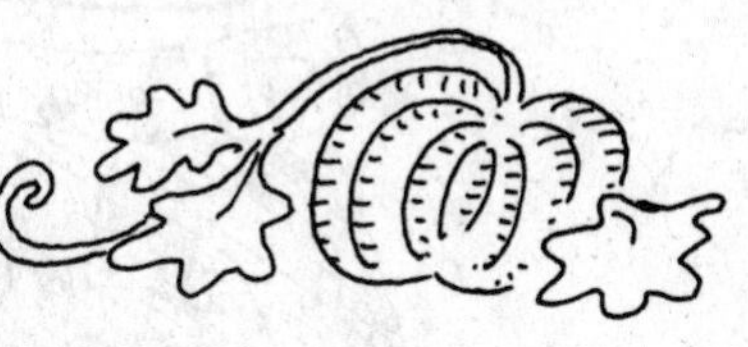

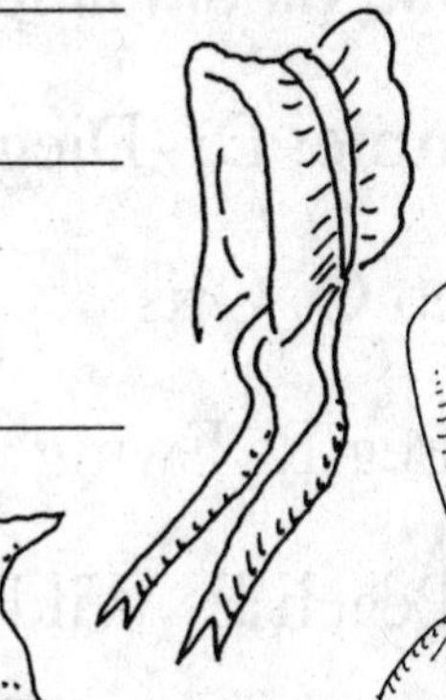

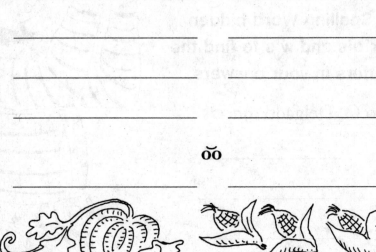

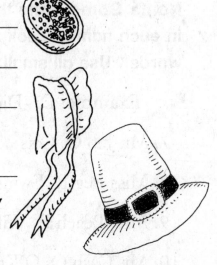

Name ______________________________

Spelling Spree

Puzzle Play **Write a Spelling Word to fit each clue.**

1. a color __ [ ] __ __
2. a toy you blow up __ [ ] __ __ __ __ __
3. not a fork or a knife __ __ __ __ [ ]
4. past tense of *draw* [ ] __ __ __
5. a dentist works on it __ __ __ __ [ ]
6. to prepare food by heating __ [ ] __ __

What two words might someone on a ship be glad to hear? To find out, write the boxed letters in order.

__ __ __ __   __ __!

Spelling Words

1. tooth
2. chew
3. grew
4. cook
5. shoe*
6. blue*
7. boot
8. flew
9. shook
10. balloon
11. drew
12. spoon

Name Game **Write the Spelling Word hidden in each name. Look for *o*'s and *w*'s to find the words. Use all small letters in your answers.**

Example: Dr. Diego O. Delgado ***good***

7. Mr. Jeb O. Otis ______________
8. Miss Peg R. Ewing ______________
9. Mrs. Peach E. Wild ______________
10. Mr. Cash O. O'Krook ______________

Across the Wide Dark Sea: The Mayflower Journey

Spelling The Vowel Sounds in *tooth* and *cook*

Name ______________________________

Proofreading and Writing

Proofreading Circle the four misspelled Spelling Words in this diary entry. Then write each word correctly.

This morning, we had fine sailing weather. Never have I seen a sky so clear and blew. Sister and I sat on the deck. We drew pictures of the ship and the sea. Time just floo by! Later, the sails shuk with a sudden wind, and we were sent below. I lost a shue on the stairs as I ran. I will look for it when the storm has passed.

Spelling Words

1. tooth
2. chew
3. grew
4. cook
5. shoe*
6. blue*
7. boot
8. flew
9. shook
10. balloon
11. drew
12. spoon

1. ____________
2. ____________
3. ____________
4. ____________

Write a Travel Poster The Pilgrims traveled from England to America. Have you taken an interesting trip? Did you travel by ship, car, bus, or plane? What did you see and do?

On a separate sheet of paper, write a travel poster. Make readers want to visit the place you are telling about. Use Spelling Words from the list.

Name ___________________________

Match Words and Syllables

Use the dictionary entries to answer each question below.

desperate *adjective* **1.** Without or nearly without hope.
2. Ready to run any risk because of feeling hopeless.
des•per•ate (**dĕs'** pər ĭt) ◇ *adjective*

friend *noun* **1.** A person one knows, likes, and enjoys being with. **2.** Someone who supports a group, cause, or movement.
friend (frĕnd) ◇ *noun, plural* **friends**

1. Which word contains one syllable? ___________________
2. Which word contains three syllables? ___________________
3. Which word contains one syllable with two vowels? ___________________
4. What is the first syllable of the word *desperate*? ___________________
5. Show where the word *desperate* can be hyphenated for word breaks.

____

Name ____________________

Using Pronouns for Nouns

Circle each subject pronoun in the following paragraph. Then write each pronoun and the verb it matches on the lines below the paragraph.

The anchor rises from the sea. It drips water. Father looks at the ocean. He hopes the journey will be safe. The sailors cheer. They want the journey to begin. I hold my mother's hand. We feel nervous and excited.

1. ____________________
2. ____________________
3. ____________________
4. ____________________
5. ____________________

Choose the correct verb to complete each sentence.

6. I ____________________ the wind in our sail. (watch, watches)
7. It ____________________ my hair. (blow, blows)
8. We ____________________ to the sailors. (shout, shouts)
9. They ____________________ our call. (answer, answers)
10. You ____________________ the sound of waves. (hear, hears)

Name ______________________________

Replacing Nouns with Pronouns

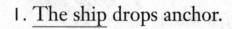

Rewrite each sentence. Replace each underlined subject with a subject pronoun.

1. The ship drops anchor.

____

2. Father points to our new home.

____

3. The workers build rough houses.

____

4. Mother nurses the sick.

____

5. The weather is harsh and dangerous.

____

6. My brother and I take care of the young children.

____

7. Mother and Father protect our home.

____

8. The fields turn green in May.

____

9. The sun shines across the land.

____

10. Mother, Father, my brother, and I watch the sunrise.

____

Name ________________________

Combining Sentences with Pronouns

Sentence Combining with Subject Pronouns Combine each pair of sentences. Use the word in parentheses.

1. You talk to the captain. I talk to the captain. (and)

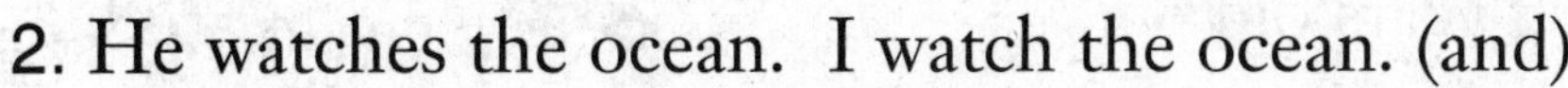

2. He watches the ocean. I watch the ocean. (and)

____

3. She helps the sailors. I help the sailors. (and)

____

4. They sleep on deck. I sleep on deck. (and)

____

5. You feel the cold wind. They feel the cold wind. (and)

____

6. He raises the sail. I raise the sail. (and)

____

7. He steers the boat. She steers the boat. (or)

____

8. You will wake up first. She will wake up first. (or)

____

9. He builds the house. She builds the house. (and)

____

10. You plant the corn. I plant the corn. (or)

____

Name ______________________________

Writing a Scene from a Play

Title: The Wide Dark Sea

Scene 1: Time — November 1620
Place — a beach in the new land

Characters
Thomas — a boy about 8 years old
William — his brother, a boy about 6 years old

What Happens in This Scene

The two boys race up and down the beach. They find clams and mussels and eat them raw. They eat too many and then feel sick.

How the Boys Feel

They are happy to be off the ship. They are excited about the beach. They also are glad to eat fresh food like the clams and mussels. When they feel sick, they are sorry they ate too much.

Play-act with a partner and pretend to be one of the two boys. Act out the events under **What Happens in This Scene**. Remember to show how the boys feel about each event.

Make notes on this page for dialogue and action ideas. Then write your scene on another sheet of paper.

____

____

____

____

Name ______________________________

Exclamation Points

Read the play scene. Add exclamation points where they belong.

Scene: Place: The Pilgrim settlement on Cape Cod
Time: A spring day in 1621

Mother: It has been a long, terrible winter. But now it is spring. Our family has survived. I am so happy.

Father: Now the children can go outside and play. (*The two children run for the door.*) Watch out, Nathan and Sarah. You almost knocked over that table.

Nathan: *(excitedly)* The sun is shining. I'll bet it's warm out.

Sarah: *(shouting)* Look, Nathan. There are birds in that tree, and they're making a nest.

Mother: Please calm down, children. Eat your breakfast. Then you can go out to play.

Father: I am so thankful that we have made it to this new land.

Now write a sentence of your own using an exclamation point.

____

____

____

____

Name ______________________________

Revising Your Description

Reread your description. Put a checkmark in the box for each sentence that describes your paper. Use this page to help you revise.

Rings the Bell

- ☐ The beginning clearly tells what the description is about.
- ☐ Details tell what I saw, heard, tasted, smelled, or touched. They are clearly ordered.
- ☐ I used sensory words for at least three of the five senses.
- ☐ Readers can easily tell how I feel about the topic.
- ☐ My sentences start differently. There are few mistakes.

Getting Stronger

- ☐ The beginning could be clearer about what the topic is.
- ☐ I need more details. I could order them more clearly.
- ☐ I need sensory words. I need to write about more senses.
- ☐ Readers can't always tell how I feel about the topic.
- ☐ Most sentences sound the same. I made some mistakes.

Try Harder

- ☐ The beginning doesn't say what the description is about.
- ☐ There are few details. The order is confusing.
- ☐ I didn't use any sensory words. I wrote using only one of my senses.
- ☐ Readers won't have any idea how I feel about the topic.
- ☐ All sentences sound the same. I made many mistakes.

Name ______________________________

Complete Sentences

Write the words *Complete Sentence* after each complete sentence. Make each incomplete sentence complete by adding words.

1. San Francisco is America's most hilly town.

____

2. Is located right next to the Golden Gate Bridge.

____

3. Some of the hills.

____

4. Going down the hills in a car or cable car can seem scary.

____

5. Lombard Street goes back and forth and back and forth.

____

6. Is the most crooked street in the city.

____

Name ______________________________

Spelling Words

Look for spelling patterns you have learned to help you remember the Spelling Words on this page. Think about the parts that you find hard to spell.

Write the missing letters in the Spelling Words below.

1. d ____ ____ n
2. h ____ ____
3. i ____ ____
4. com ____ ____ ____
5. sto ____ ____ ed
6. st ____ ____ ____ ____ ____
7. ____ ____ ote
8. swi ____ ____ ing
9. fr ____ m
10. ____ ____ ite
11. wri ____ ____ ng
12. br ____ ____ ____ ____ t

Spelling Words

1. down
2. how
3. its
4. coming
5. stopped
6. started
7. wrote
8. swimming
9. from
10. write
11. writing
12. brought

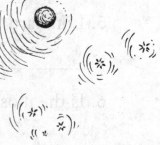

Study List On another sheet of paper, write each Spelling Word. Check the list to be sure you spell each word correctly.

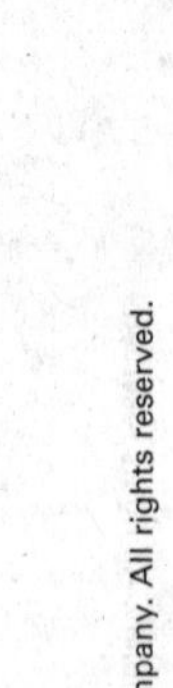

Name ____________________

Spelling Spree

Find a Rhyme Write a Spelling Word that rhymes with the underlined word.

1. Last night I had to ____________ a report on Mars.
2. Jamie ____________ home the fish he caught.
3. The statue sits in ____________ own room in the museum.
4. Do you know ____________ to milk a cow?
5. The teacher ____________ me a note to give to my parents.
6. These apples come ____________ Washington.
7. I sat ____________ in my seat just as a clown came on stage.

Spelling Words

1. down
2. how
3. its
4. coming
5. stopped
6. started
7. wrote
8. swimming
9. from
10. write
11. writing
12. brought

Meaning Match Each exercise gives a clue for a word along with an ending. Add the base to the ending to write a Spelling Word. Remember that the spelling of the first word may change.

8. to put words on paper + *ing*
9. to begin + *ed*
10. to move toward the person speaking + *ing*
11. to end + *ed*
12. what you do in a pool + *ing*

8. ____________
9. ____________
10. ____________
11. ____________
12. ____________

Name ______________________________

Proofreading and Writing

Proofreading **Circle the four misspelled Spelling Words in this diary entry. Then write each word correctly.**

May 3rd

Things are going pretty well, except that I'm busy with homework. We have to rite a report on an explorer for school. I startted writing mine last week. I was going to finish it on Monday, but we went swiming instead. Now it's due in two days, and I have to figure out howe to finish it on time. I'll be glad when I'm done.

Spelling Words

1. down
2. how
3. its
4. coming
5. stopped
6. started
7. wrote
8. swimming
9. from
10. write
11. writing
12. brought

1. ____________________
2. ____________________
3. ____________________
4. ____________________

Write a Round-Robin Story **Get together in a small group with other students. Then write a story about a voyage, with each of you writing one sentence at a time. Use a Spelling Word from the list in each sentence.**

Name ______________________________

Travel Words

Match each word with its definition by writing the letter of the definition on the line beside the word. Then choose a vocabulary word from the list to finish each sentence.

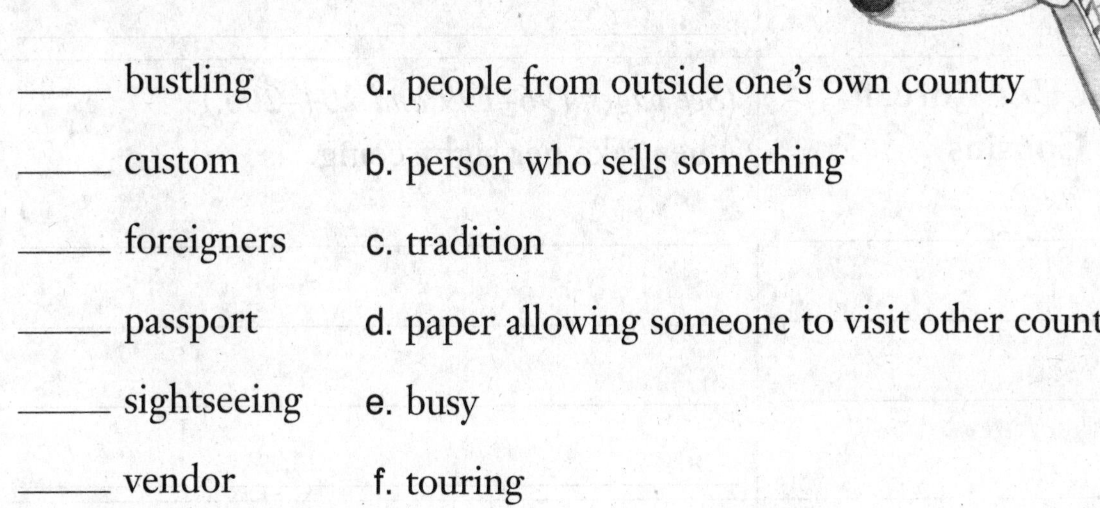

_____ bustling   a. people from outside one's own country

_____ custom   b. person who sells something

_____ foreigners   c. tradition

_____ passport   d. paper allowing someone to visit other countries

_____ sightseeing   e. busy

_____ vendor   f. touring

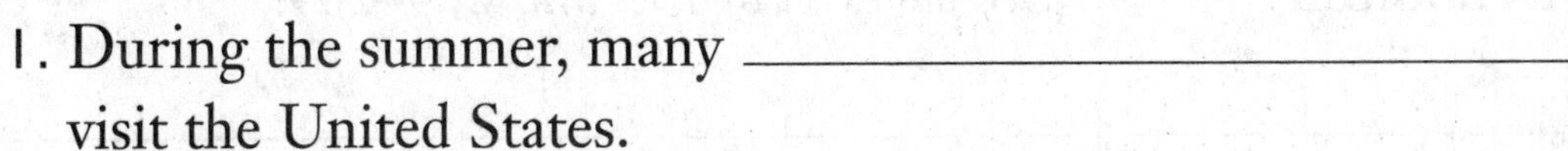

1. During the summer, many ______________________ visit the United States.
2. Each traveler needs to bring a ______________________ in order to enter the country.
3. In New York City, the streets are usually ______________________ with people.
4. Many of the people are tourists going ______________________.
5. On some streets, they can buy hot dogs and other snacks from a ______________________.
6. In America, it is the ______________________ to shake hands with people you meet.

Name ______________________

Character Chart

Yunmi's Feelings	Story Clues
About Her Visit to Korea excited anxious	*(See page 190.)* ______________________ ______________________
About Her Korean Cousins ______________________ ______________________ ______________________ jealous	*(See pages 196–199 and 204–206.)* They take her sightseeing. ______________________ ______________________ ______________________ ______________________
About Halmoni ______________________ ______________________ ashamed about being selfish	*(See pages 198–199 and 203–205.)* ______________________ ______________________ ______________________ ______________________ ______________________

What do you think Yunmi will do if her cousins come to visit her in New York? Explain why you think as you do.

____

____

Name ______________________________

Finish the Letter

Suppose Yunmi wrote this letter. Write story details to finish her letter.

Dear Anna Marie,

We've had a wonderful time in Korea! When ______________________________ and I first arrived at the airport, I had to stand in the line for ______________________________. That made me feel strange. However, my Korean family made me feel welcome. I loved sightseeing and shopping, and my cousins Jinhi and Sunhi helped me ______________________________. For a time I became sad, because I thought that my grandmother ______________________________. Then we went to my grandfather's gravesite to ______________________________. That's where Halmoni told me that she would be ______________________________.

Next year I hope that my cousins will come to New York for a visit. You can help me take them sightseeing! I'll be home soon, and I can't wait to see you.

Your friend,
Yunmi

Name ______________________

Other Outcomes

Read the story. Then complete the chart on the next page.

Ando's Journey

Long ago in Japan, Ando loved to draw. He knew that one day he must follow in his father's footsteps. He must become head firefighter at the castle, as was the custom. But Ando loved to draw.

When Ando was twelve, his mother died. The next year, his father died, so Ando started to work. But he missed drawing so much that he set out to find a teacher. He had to study art.

Ando's first choice was a very famous artist. He begged the artist to help him, but the man simply turned him down, as did many others. Finally, Ando found Toyohiro, a quiet artist who loved nature and made woodblock prints. Ando learned to love nature and make prints much as his teacher did. Ando's work was so beautiful that he helped make this new art style popular.

One day, Ando left for a long journey through Japan. He began drawing everything he saw — mountains, water, the boats in the harbor, people flying kites or drinking tea. Then he turned his pictures into woodblock prints. More than fifty years later, artists in Europe saw a collection of his works. The prints gave them new ideas on drawing and painting.

Name ______________________________

Other Outcomes continued

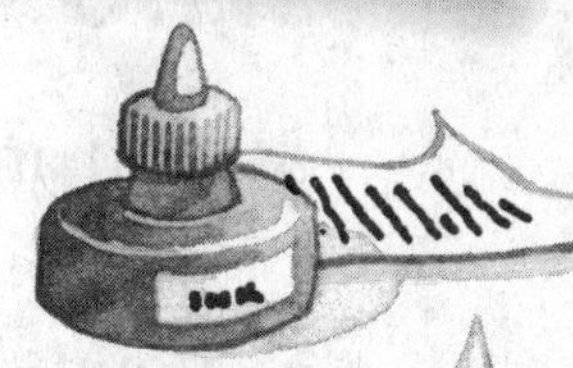

Answer each question by predicting an outcome. Then give reasons why you think as you do.

1. What if Ando's parents had not died when he was young?

Predicted Outcome

____

Reasons

____

____

2. What if Ando had never found Toyohiro?

Predicted Outcome

____

Reasons

____

____

3. What would have been the outcome if Ando had liked to stay home instead of travel?

Predicted Outcome

____

Reasons

____

____

Name ______________________________

Who Owns It?

► Add an **apostrophe** and *s ('s)* to a singular noun to make it show ownership. Add an **apostrophe** *(')* to a plural noun that already ends with *s* to make it show ownership.

Halmoni**'s** hand   parents**'** names

Complete each sentence. Add an apostrophe and s or just an apostrophe to make each noun in dark type show ownership. The first one is done for you.

Last weekend, my family went to visit my **(mother)** mother's sister. **(Aunt Jenny)** ______________ house is three hours away. I carried my two little **(sisters)** ______________ bags out to the car. I couldn't lift my **(parents)** ______________ suitcases because they were too heavy.

I was very excited to see my cousins. My **(cousins)** ______________ names are Ryan and Marie. As soon as my family got there, Ryan and Marie took me to their pet **(rabbits)** ______________ cages behind the house. **(Ryan)** ______________ rabbit is named Flopsy. **(Flopsy)** ______________ ears hang straight down. **(Marie)** ______________ rabbit is named Topsy. **(Topsy)** ______________ ears stick straight up. This time there was a surprise — a rabbit for me! My new **(rabbit)** ______________ name is Mopsy.

Name ______________________________

The Vowel Sound in *bought*

When you hear the /ô/ sound, remember that it can be spelled with the pattern *ough* or *augh*.

/ô/ **bought, caught**

► In the starred words *laugh*, *through*, *enough*, and *cough*, the *ough* and *augh* patterns spell other sounds.

Write each Spelling Word under its *ough* or *augh* spelling pattern.

Spelling Words

1. caught
2. thought
3. bought
4. laugh*
5. through*
6. enough*
7. fought
8. daughter
9. taught
10. brought
11. ought
12. cough*

______________________ ______________________

______________________ ______________________

______________________ ______________________

______________________ ______________________

______________________ ______________________

______________________ ______________________

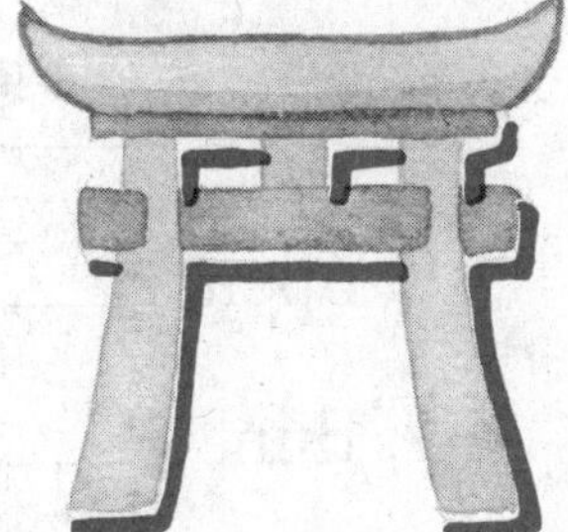

Name ______________________________

Spelling Spree

Only Opposites Write the Spelling Word that is the opposite of each clue.

1. not sold, but ______________________
2. not learned, but ______________________
3. not dropped, but ______________________
4. not took, but ______________________
5. not son, but ______________________
6. not cry, but ______________________

Spelling Words

1. caught
2. thought
3. bought
4. laugh*
5. through*
6. enough*
7. fought
8. daughter
9. taught
10. brought
11. ought
12. cough*

Alphabet Puzzler Write the Spelling Word that goes in ABC order between each pair of words.

7. cool, _____, daze
8. open, _____, paste
9. thin, _____, thunder
10. find, _____, game

7. ______________________
8. ______________________
9. ______________________
10. ______________________

Name ______________________

Proofreading and Writing

Proofreading Suppose Yunmi sent this note. Circle the five misspelled Spelling Words in it. Then write each word correctly.

Dear Mom and Dad,

Halmoni and I are here in Korea! I thoght the plane ride was really neat. Everyone loves the presents we brought. We went throogh a palace today. I hope we have enouf time to see everything. Halmoni has baught some gifts for you. You will laugh when you see them!

Your loving dauter,

Yunmi

Spelling Words

1. caught
2. thought
3. bought
4. laugh*
5. through*
6. enough*
7. fought
8. daughter
9. taught
10. brought
11. ought
12. cough*

1. ______________
2. ______________
3. ______________
4. ______________
5. ______________

Write an Opinion An **opinion** tells what you believe or feel about something. Think of two places you have visited. Did you like one place better than the other? Why?

On a separate sheet of paper, write an opinion. Tell about the places you visited, and explain why you liked one place better than the other. Use Spelling Words from the list.

Name ______________________________

Everything in Its Place

Read the first pair of words in each analogy below. Decide how the words are related. Then write the word that best completes the analogy.

1. **Author** is to **book** as **painter** is to ______________________.
   brush picture artist
2. **Breakfast** is to **dinner** as **morning** is to ______________________.
   sun toast evening
3. **Scissors** is to **cut** as **pencil** is to ______________________.
   write yellow crayon
4. **Twelve** is to **number** as **green** is to ______________________.
   grass color shape
5. **Bee** is to **honey** as **hen** is to ______________________.
   egg corn farm
6. **Rude** is to **polite** as **dishonest** is to ______________________.
   calm mean honest
7. **Television** is to **watch** as **radio** is to ______________________.
   listen screen volume
8. **Frog** is to **tadpole** as **butterfly** is to ______________________.
   pretty caterpillar flying

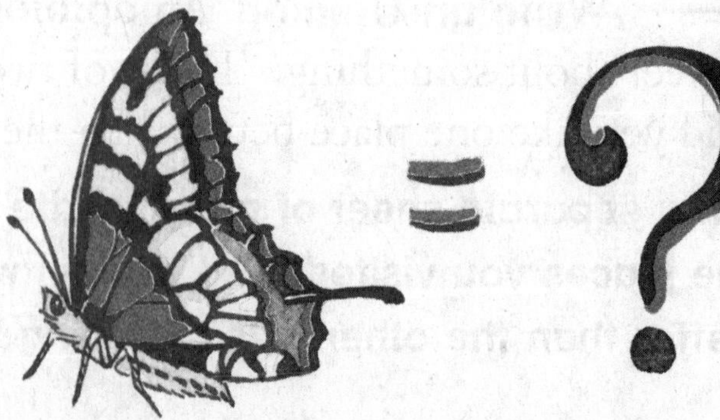

Name ______________________________

Circling Object Pronouns

Circle each object pronoun in the paragraph below. Then write the object pronouns on the lines below the paragraph.

Sunhi shows Yunmi how to make dumplings. She gives her a thin dumpling skin and some filling. Yunmi rolls it. She places the new dumpling on a tray with the other dumplings. The girls take them to the picnic. They share the dumplings with us. Yunmi gives one to me to taste.

1. ____________________ 4. ____________________

2. ____________________ 5. ____________________

3. ____________________

Choose the correct word or phrase in parentheses to complete each sentence.

6. The picnic is a special event for __________. (we, us)
7. Yunmi tells __________ about life in New York. (they, them)
8. Halmoni tells __________ a story. (her, she)
9. Her voice makes __________ feel better. (me, I)
10. The picnic made ____________________ very happy. (me and Halmoni, Halmoni and me)

Name ______________________________

Rewriting with Object Pronouns

Object Pronouns	
Singular	**Plural**
me you him, her, it	us you them

Rewrite each sentence. Replace each underlined word or phrase with an object pronoun.

1. The airplane takes Halmoni and Yunmi to Korea.

____

2. Yunmi shows her passport to the man.

____

3. Outside the airport, Yunmi hugs her cousins.

____

4. Yunmi buys the purse for Helen.

____

5. Halmoni takes Yunmi and her cousins to the National Museum.

____

Name ______________________________

Using the Correct Pronoun

What if Yunmi sent her friend this postcard? Circle any pronouns that are used incorrectly. Then rewrite the postcard.

Dear Helen,

Korea is wonderful. Halmoni and me arrived last week. Her showed me many wonderful sights. Us went to the National Museum with my cousins, Sunhi and Jinhi. Them took us to a market too. One vendor sold bean cakes. Sunhi and I picked out this card.

Halmoni showed I and Sunhi how to make dumplings. I will be home soon. Me and you will make some dumplings!

Bye,
Yunmi

____

____

____

____

____

____

____

____

____

Name ______________________________

Writing a Message

Use this page to take a message.

Date: ____________________ Time: ____________________

For: ____

From: ______________ Telephone number: ______________

Message: ____

____

____

____

____

____

____

____

Message taken by: ______________________________

MESSAGES

Name ______________________________

Using Complete Information

Suppose Yunmi and Halmoni each made a phone call. "Listen" to each answering machine and read the message. Make the messages complete by adding any missing information.

1. Hi, Halmoni, it's Yunmi. It's 3:00 on Monday. Junhi and I are going to the park. We will be home at 5:30. If you need us, you can call Mr. Choi's market at 333-6748. He will get the message to us.

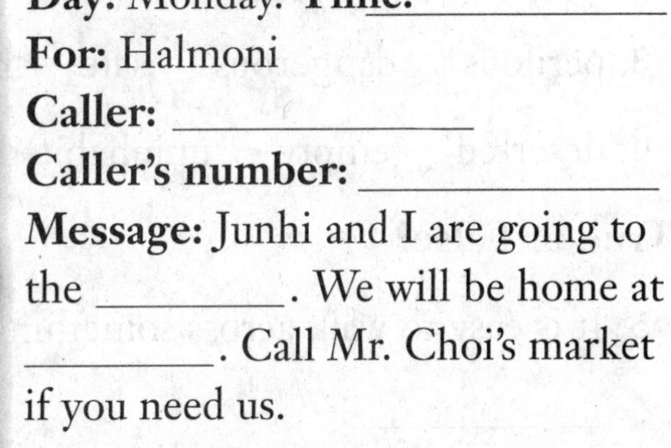

Day: Monday. **Time:** ____________
For: Halmoni
Caller: ____________
Caller's number: ____________
Message: Junhi and I are going to the ________. We will be home at ________. Call Mr. Choi's market if you need us.

2. Hello, Junhi and Sunhi. This is Halmoni, on Tuesday at 11:30. I want you to teach Yunmi how to make mandoo on Wednesday afternoon. I'll be home to help you. Leave a message for me at 333-2135.

Day: ________ **Time:** 11:30
For: Junhi ________________
Caller: Halmoni
Caller's number: 333-2135
Message: Teach Yunmi how to make mandoo ________________ ________ I'll be home to help you. Leave a message for me at ________________.

Name ______________________________

Selection Vocabulary

Cross out the word that doesn't belong.

1. terrain earth sky land
2. grueling resting tiring difficult
3. perilous dangerous safe risky
4. deserted empty uninhabited bustling

True or False?

5. It is easy to walk across something impassable.

____

6. Ice sheets floating on water are called floes.

____

7. Land that is barren has many plants and animals.

____

8. A crevasse is a deep crack.

____

Name ______________________________

Text Organization Chart

Text Feature	Where It Is	Purpose
heading (date)		
photograph, caption, illustration		
definition		
chronological sequence		

Name ______________________________

Shackleton Survives!

Complete the news report by adding the missing information.

Sir Ernest Shackleton and his crew survived many hardships on their recent voyage to ____________________. Hundreds of miles from land, their ship, the ____________________, became ____________________. The men camped for months on slowly moving ____________________. When they reached open water, they set out in lifeboats on a perilous voyage to ____________________.

There, the men split up. Shackleton and five others sailed on toward ____________________. The six men finally landed. Shackleton and two others hiked across tall ____________________ to get to a ____________________, where they hoped to find ____________________. On May 20, 1916, the three exhausted men reached safety, but the voyage did not really end until more than three months later, when Shackleton ______________________________ ______________________________.

Name ______________________________

Organized Hike

Read this news story. Then complete the chart on the next page.

Hiker Stranded

Lost

7:00 P.M. on April 1: Donald McCarthy, 53, of Keene, New Hampshire, got lost while hiking along an old logging trail near Waterville Valley. (A logging trail is used by workers who take away cut trees.) By nightfall, McCarthy knew he would have to spend the night in the woods.

. . . and Found

8:00 P.M.: A Fish and Game officer thought he spotted McCarthy and called out. McCarthy never answered, and the officer moved on. The next morning, McCarthy was found. When questioned by Fish and Game, McCarthy admitted he thought he heard someone call, but he also heard noises in the brush. "I was sure it was a bear," McCarthy said, "so I kept quiet and climbed into a tree for the night."

Bear Sighted
in Area:
Use Caution

This sign led McCarthy into thinking he heard bears.

Name ______________________________

Organized Hike continued

Finish the chart with text features from "Hiker Stranded." Explain the purpose of each feature.

Example of Text Feature	Purpose of the Text Feature
Heading ________________ ________________	________________ ________________
Caption ________________ ________________	________________ ________________
Definition ________________ ________________	________________ ________________
Chronological sequence (dates, times) ________________ ________________	________________ ________________

If you were a reporter, what other information would you add? What text feature would you use to give more information?

____

____

Name ______________________________

VCCV Challenge

Write the VCCV word that matches each clue in the puzzle. Use the Word Bank and a dictionary for help.

Across

1. soaking wet
6. wood used for building
7. the coldest season
8. captain of a ship
9. to save from danger

Down

1. the peak of a mountain
2. cloth used for making tents or sails
3. an Antarctic bird
4. a long trip
5. to remain alive

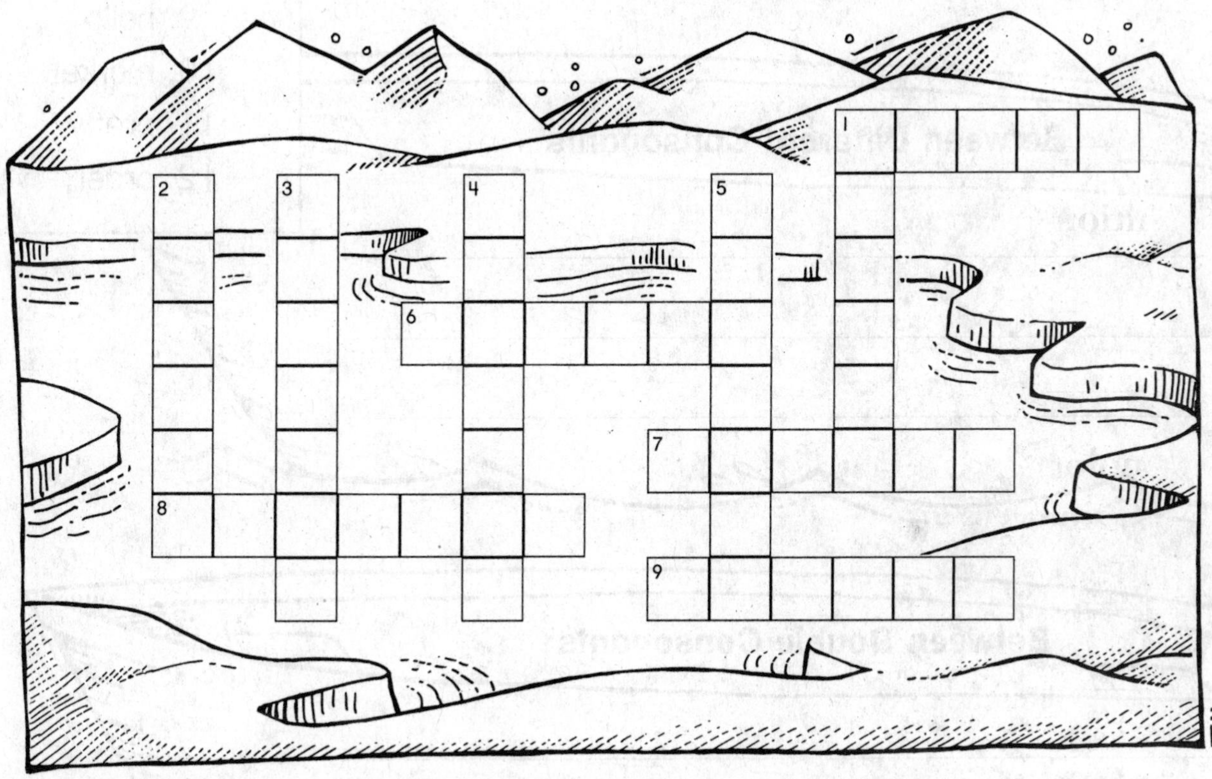

canvas	lumber	penguin	soggy	skipper
journey	winter	rescue	survive	summit

Name ______________________

The VCCV Pattern

To spell a word with the VCCV pattern, divide the word between the two consonants. Look for spelling patterns you have learned. Spell the word by syllables.

vc|cv **vc|cv**

Mon | day  sud | den

Write each Spelling Word under the head that tells where the word is divided into syllables.

Spelling Words

1. Monday
2. sudden
3. until
4. forget
5. happen
6. follow
7. dollar
8. window
9. hello
10. market
11. pretty
12. order

Name ______________________

Spelling Spree

Silly Statements Each statement was made by a South Pole visitor. Write the Spelling Word that best completes each sentence.

Spelling Words

1. Monday
2. sudden
3. until
4. forget
5. happen
6. follow
7. dollar
8. window
9. hello
10. market
11. pretty
12. order

1. I will not sell my mittens for a ______.
2. I won't go home ______ I've seen a whale.
3. A seal just tried to climb through my ______.
4. I said ______ to the iceberg as it passed.
5. Please run to the ______ to buy some oranges.
6. That polar bear keeps trying to ______ me around.
7. The little bird in the tux will take your ______.

1. ______________________
2. ______________________
3. ______________________
4. ______________________
5. ______________________
6. ______________________
7. ______________________

Name ______________________________

Proofreading and Writing

Proofreading Circle the five misspelled Spelling Words in this script. Then write each word correctly.

Sam: We are leaving Mondy for a trip to the South Pole.

Emma: Wow! I didn't know that. Is this a suddin trip?

Sam: No, we've been planning it for ages. I hear it's a really pritty place.

Emma: If you hapen to see any penguins, say hello for me.

Sam: Sure. If you want me to say hi to a killer whale, though, you can ferget it!

Spelling Words

1. Monday
2. sudden
3. until
4. forget
5. happen
6. follow
7. dollar
8. window
9. hello
10. market
11. pretty
12. order

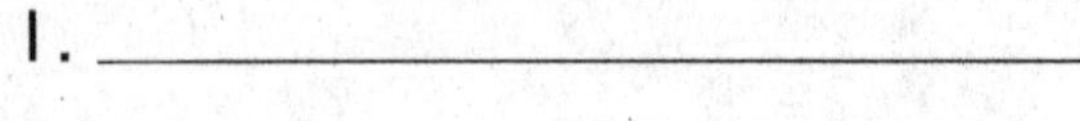

1. ______________________
2. ______________________
3. ______________________
4. ______________________
5. ______________________

Write a List How would you prepare for a trip to the South Pole? Would you need to buy things? If so, what? Where would you buy the goods?

On a separate sheet of paper, write a list of things to do to get ready for a trip to the South Pole. Use Spelling Words from the list.

Name ______________________

Sounds the Same

From the word box below, choose a pair of homophones to complete each pair of sentences. Choose the spelling that fits the meaning of the sentence and write it in the blank. Use a dictionary if you are not sure which is which.

not	one	see	threw	bear
knot	won	sea	through	bare

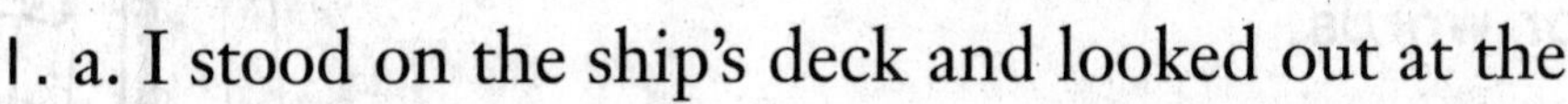

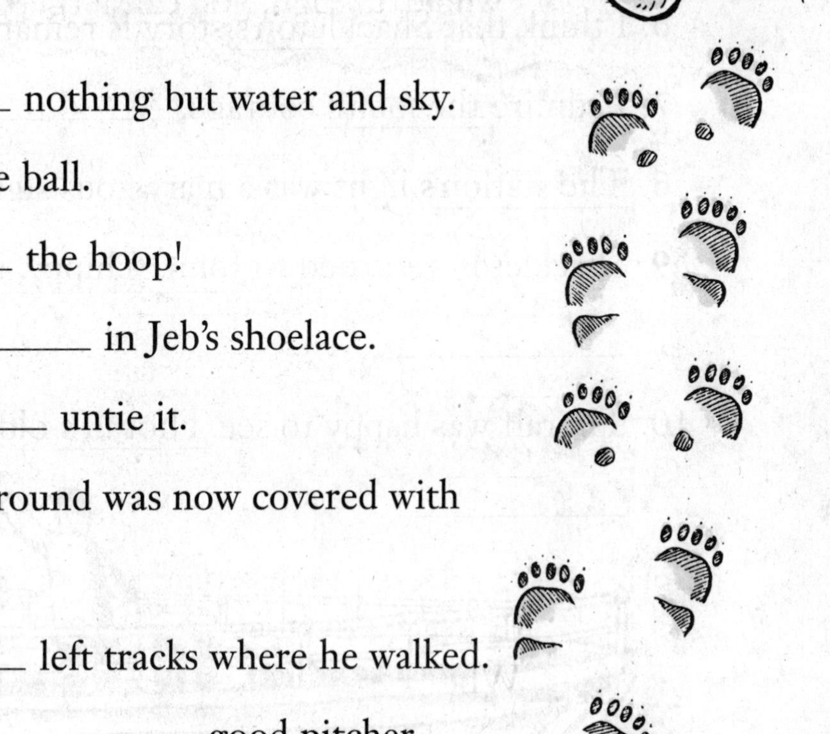

1. a. I stood on the ship's deck and looked out at the ______________.

   b. I could ______________ nothing but water and sky.

2. a. Jen ______________ the ball.

   b. It went ______________ the hoop!

3. a. There was a ______________ in Jeb's shoelace.

   b. He could ______________ untie it.

4. a. The ______________ ground was now covered with snow.

   b. The big ______________ left tracks where he walked.

5. a. Our team has only ______________ good pitcher.

   b. Even so, we have ______________ every game.

Name ______________________________

Writing Possessively

Write the possessive pronoun in each sentence.

1. The men began their voyage in 1915. ____________
2. Shackleton and his crew were very brave. ____________
3. Our class read about the amazing adventure. ____________
4. I asked my teacher about ice floes. ____________
5. Her explanation was clear and helpful. ____________

Write the possessive pronoun that could take the place of the underlined word or words.

6. I think that Shackleton's story is remarkable. ____________
7. I admire the men's courage. ____________
8. The station's light was a marvelous sight. ____________
9. Shackleton returned to John, Chippy, and Tim's camp.

   ____

10. Thoralf was happy to see Thoralf's old friend.

   ____

Name ________________________________

Choosing Possessives

Choose the correct word in parentheses to complete each sentence.

1. Shackleton led ____________ crew to Antarctica. (him, his)
2. The *Endurance* was a useless hulk, lying on ____________ side. (it's, its)
3. The men carried ____________ food with them. (they, their)
4. ____________ journey was just beginning. (Their, There)
5. Shackleton described ____________ plan. (he's, his)
6. The lifeboats were ____________ only hope. (their, they're)
7. Each boat had ____________ own sled. (its, its')
8. ____________ class studied the perilous trip. (Our, Ours)
9. I decided to write ____________ story about Antarctica. (me, my)
10. Is ____________ story about Shackleton? (your, you)

Name ______________________________

Writing a Story

Alana wrote a story about Shackleton's crew. Proofread Alana's writing. Check that *its* and *it's* are used correctly. Then rewrite the letter on the lines below.

May 19, 1916

Its very cold again today. John and Chippy are still very ill. The sun is bright, but it's light brings no heat. This barren land is deserted and lonely.

I explored the terrain yesterday. Its difficult to follow a trail. At last, I killed a seal. It's meat will feed us for several days. The food is so cold it has lost it's taste.

I hope that Shackleton and the others can survive their journey. Its hard to imagine a more grueling adventure.

____

____

____

____

____

____

____

____

____

Name ______________________________

A Learning Log Entry

Pick two examples of your own writing. Carefully reread your work. Complete the Learning Log entry. List what you have learned under *What I Learned.* List what needs more work under *My Goals.*

LEARNING LOG

Writing sample 1: ____________________ Date: __________

Writing sample 2: ____________________ Date: __________

What I Learned:	**My Goals:**
____________________	____________________
____________________	____________________
____________________	____________________
____________________	____________________
____________________	____________________
____________________	____________________
____________________	____________________
____________________	____________________

Name ______________________________

Using Dates and Times

► Dates are written: Month, day, year. A comma separates the day and year. Dates can also be written in numerals with slash marks.

The fifth of February in 2003: February 5, 2003
or 2/5/03

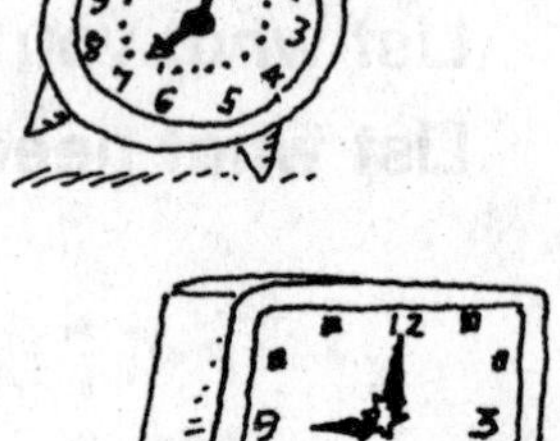

► A.M. stands for morning, from one minute after midnight until noon. Seven o'clock in the morning: 7:00 A.M.

► P.M. stands for after noon, from one minute after noon until midnight. Nine o'clock in the evening: 9:00 P.M.

Write each date two ways.

1. The seventh day of April in 2011

_______________ _______________

2. The thirty-first of October in 2006

_______________ _______________

Write each time.

3. Six-fifteen (after noon)

____

4. Eight thirty-five (morning)

____

5. Ten minutes after ten (morning)

____

6. Forty minutes after nine (after noon)

____

Name ______________________________

Words for Ocean Voyagers

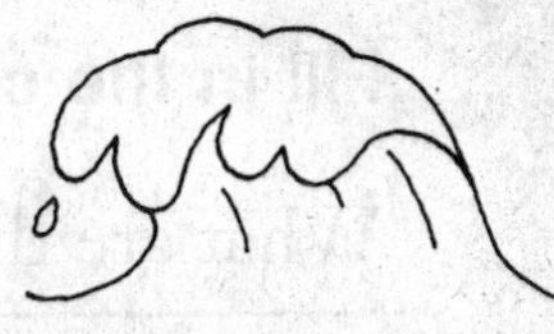

In the box above each word, draw a picture that shows the meaning of the word. Then answer the questions below.

1. harpoons	2. calabashes	3. hull

4. What might give you a feeling of **awe**?

____

____

5. If the waves were **roiling**, would you want to go swimming? Why or why not?

____

____

6. Why would you want to make sure a boat was **seaworthy** before sailing on it?

____

Monitoring Student Progress

Graphic Organizer Making Inferences

Name ____________________

Inference Chart

Fill in the chart as you read the stories.

What are the voyagers in these stories like?

Characters	What the Characters Do	What I Know	My Inference
Manu in *The Island-below-the-Star*			
Bud and Temple in *A Wild Ride* 			

How are the voyagers in these stories alike? How are they different?

Name ____________________

What Happens Next?

Make predictions about what will happen to Manu after the end of *The Island-below-the-Star.* Support each prediction with details from the story. Then choose another selection in Theme 5 to complete the chart.

	Manu in *The Island-below-the-Star*	**Character: ______ Story Title: ______**
Will the character go back home, or stay at the trip's destination?		
What details make you think so?		
How will the character's life be different after this journey?		
What details make you think so?		
Will the character travel again, or not?		
What details make you think so?		

Monitoring
Student Progress

Key Vocabulary

Name ______________________

Safe at Last!

Use words from the box to complete the news article below.

Vocabulary

territory
slogging
newsreel

Heroes Survive the Mountains

A group of climbers has survived being lost for a week in the wilderness. The group got lost during a snowstorm in Yellowstone National Park. This area of land is ______________ controlled by the United States Park Service.

After six days of ______________ through heavy snow, the group was rescued by plane. For more details on this amazing story, watch the ______________ that will soon be coming to a movie theater near you!

Now write your own sentences using the Key Vocabulary words. Use one Vocabulary word in each sentence.

1. ______________________________

____

2. ______________________________

____

3. ______________________________

____

Monitoring Student Progress

Taking Tests Writing an Answer to a Question

Name ________________________________

Test Practice

Use the three steps you've learned to write an answer to these questions about *A Wild Ride.* Make a chart on a separate piece of paper, and write your answer on the lines below. Use the checklist to revise your answer.

1. In what way does the title of the story *A Wild Ride* describe the trip that Bud and Temple Abernathy took?

____

____

____

____

____

____

____

____

____

____

Checklist For Writing an Answer to a Question

✔ Did I restate the question at the beginning?

✔ Can I add more details from what I read to support my answer?

✔ Do I need to delete extra details that do not help answer the question?

✔ Did I write carefully? Did I make any mistakes?

Continued on page 140.

Name ______________________

Test Practice continued

2. **Connecting/Comparing** Two brothers take a cross-country trip to meet Theodore Roosevelt in *A Wild Ride*. Five brothers sail to a distant island in *The Island-Below-the-Star*. How are the experiences alike?

Checklist for Writing an Answer to a Question

- ✔ Did I restate the question at the beginning?
- ✔ Can I add more details from what I read to support my answer?
- ✔ Do I need to delete extra details that do not help answer the question?
- ✔ Did I write carefully? Did I make any mistakes?

Read your answers to Questions 1 and 2 aloud to a partner. Then discuss the checklist. Make any changes that will make your answers better.

Name ______________________

Guess How I Feel

Read the passage. Then answer the questions.

March 5

Today was cold and gray, the perfect match for my mood. Carlo, Tina, and I piled into Mom's car, and I turned to get one last look at our old neighborhood. Then I squeezed my eyes shut and tried to listen to what Mom was saying.

She told us our new house would be bigger than our apartment, and it even had a yard. Mom would make more money at her new job, and she knew we'd make new friends soon.

I heard all this, but none of it helped make the lump in my throat go away.

1. How does the writer feel about moving?	
Story Clue ______________________ ______________________	What I Know ______________________ ______________________
My Inference ______________________	
2. How does Mom feel about moving?	
Story Clue ______________________ ______________________	What I Know ______________________ ______________________
My Inference ______________________	

Name ______________________________

Headings

Story headings often give a preview of the text that follows. Write the headings from *A Wild Ride* below and fill in the main idea of each section.

Heading	Main Idea of Section

Name ______________________________

Whose Is It?

Replace each underlined phrase with a phrase containing a possessive noun. Rewrite the sentence. Remember that when a plural noun ends in *s*, you only need to add an apostrophe to make it possessive.

1. Tony passed the house that belongs to the Jacksons.

____

2. The coat that belongs to Emma is red.

____

3. The wind blew the nest of the birds out of the tree.

____

4. We bought the birthday present for Mom yesterday.

____

5. The face of the teacher was kind.

____

6. The favorite food of the twins is pizza.

____

7. The kids listened to the CD that belongs to Katy.

____

8. The shoes that belong to the dancers were worn out.

____

Name ___________________________

Find the Analogy

Read the first part of each analogy below. Decide how the words in dark print are related. Then write the word that best completes the analogy.

1. **Kitten** is to **cat** as **puppy** is to ________________.
2. **Leaf** is to **green** as **snow** is to ________________.
3. **Day** is to **night** as **up** is to ________________.
4. **Scale** is to **fish** as **feather** is to ________________.
5. **Uncle** is to **aunt** as **father** is to ________________.
6. **Coach** is to **athlete** as **teacher** is to ________________.
7. **Water** is to **swim** as **ground** is to ________________.
8. **Air** is to **breathing** as **food** is to ________________.

Spelling Review

Write Spelling Words from the list on this page to answer the questions.

1–8. Which eight words have the vowel sound in **loose** or **look**?

1. ______ 5. ______
2. ______ 6. ______
3. ______ 7. ______
4. ______ 8. ______

9–15. Which seven words have the vowel sound in **fought**?

9. ______ 13. ______
10. ______ 14. ______
11. ______ 15. ______
12. ______

16–26. Which eleven words have the VCCV pattern? Hint: You have already written one of these words.

16. ______ 22. ______
17. ______ 23. ______
18. ______ 24. ______
19. ______ 25. ______
20. ______ 26. ______
21. ______

Spelling Words

1. bought
2. order
3. grew
4. hello
5. thought
6. happen
7. forget
8. caught
9. flew
10. spoon
11. daughter
12. window
13. dollar
14. brought
15. cook
16. boot
17. Monday
18. sudden
19. pretty
20. until
21. ought
22. balloon
23. chew
24. taught
25. tooth

Name ________________________

Spelling Spree

New TV Shows! **Write the Spelling Word that best completes each title of a new TV show. Remember to use capital letters.**

1. *Sook Can ____, Bake, and Roast*
2. *Look Out the ____. What Do You See?*
3. *The Superhero Who ____ Too High*
4. *Alphabetical ____: A Game Show for the Very Young*
5. *I ____ to Have Brought My Camera*
6. *A ____ Storm Springs Up in Egypt*
7. *Always ____ Your Food Well*
8. *Tongue, ____, and Throat: Have a Healthy Mouth*

Spelling Words

1. brought
2. cook
3. until
4. flew
5. tooth
6. chew
7. happen
8. ought
9. boot
10. sudden
11. order
12. spoon
13. window
14. Monday

1. ____________ 5. ____________

2. ____________ 6. ____________

3. ____________ 7. ____________

4. ____________ 8. ____________

A Strange Hike **A few words are missing from this paragraph. Use a Spelling Word to fill in each blank.**

We went hiking on 9. ____________. It had to 10. ____________ that the laces on my left 11. ____________ broke. Then we found out that no one had 12. ____________ any food. However, we did find one plastic 13. ____________. The weather was warm 14. ____________ the afternoon. That's when we went home.

Proofreading and Writing

Proofreading Circle the five misspelled Spelling Words below. Then write each word correctly.

I flew in a hot-air baloon! My uncle bot it from his friend. I never thoght it could go so high. The city looked pritty from up high. I will never fourget the ride.

1. ____________ 4. ____________

2. ____________ 5. ____________

3. ____________

Spelling Words

1. balloon
2. thought
3. grew
4. caught
5. forget
6. bought
7. pretty
8. dollar
9. until
10. taught
11. daughter
12. hello

Today's News Fix this speech. Write the Spelling Word that is the opposite of each underlined word.

Who 6. <u>learned</u> that we all should travel by car? Last year, the number of cars 7. <u>shrank</u>. Even my 8. <u>son</u> has her own car. Say good-bye to cars and 9. <u>good-bye</u> to trains! People have 10. <u>let go</u> of the excitement of train travel. If everyone gave one 11. <u>coin</u>, we could have a train tomorrow, but 12. <u>after</u> then, we won't!

6. ____________ 9. ____________ 12. ____________

7. ____________ 10. ____________

8. ____________ 11. ____________

Write a Story On another sheet of paper, write about a trip you would like to take. Use the Spelling Review Words.

Name ______________________________

Working with Subject Pronouns

Circle each subject pronoun in the following paragraph. Then write each pronoun and the verb it matches on the lines below the paragraph.

I fill my backpack with books and games. Mother packs a suitcase with clothes. We wait a long time for the van. Finally, it arrives. Mother gathers our things. We climb into the van. The driver shuts the door. Then he sits in the driver's seat and starts the engine.

1. ______________________
2. ______________________
3. ______________________
4. ______________________
5. ______________________

Write the correct verb to complete each sentence.

6. I ____________ Mother if we will be late. (ask, asks)
7. She ____________ the time of our flight. (check, checks)
8. We ____________ in plenty of time. (arrive, arrives)
9. I ____________ off, and Mother takes the suitcase from the van. (hop, hops)
10. It ____________ away. (roll, rolls)

Monitoring Student Progress

Grammar Skill Object Pronouns

Name ______________________________

Working with Object Pronouns

Circle each object pronoun in the paragraph below. Then write the object pronouns on the lines below the paragraph.

Sometimes Father cooks special foods outdoors for the family. Sis always asks him for a scallop dinner. Sis puts the scallops on little sticks called skewers. Then Father places them on the grill. Because Sis helps, the first scallops go to her. The next ones go to me. Mother makes us salad and rice to have with the scallops.

1. ______________ 4. ______________

2. ______________ 5. ______________

3. ______________

Write the correct word or phrase in parentheses to complete each sentence.

6. Sometimes Grandmother and Grandfather eat with ______________. (we, us)
7. Mother makes special place mats for ______________. (they, them)
8. They usually bring ______________ a small gift. (she, her)
9. Grandfather gave ______________ a fishing pole last week. (I, me)
10. He told ______________ about his childhood in Japan. (me and Sis, Sis and me)

Name ______________________________

Once Upon a Puzzle

Use the words from the box and the numbered clues below to complete the crossword puzzle. Then unscramble the letters below the puzzle to create the words again.

Vocabulary

fairy
heroine
hero
culture
folktale

Across

1. a traditional story handed down from one generation to the next
4. the main female character in a story, poem, or play

Down

2. a certain group's customs, beliefs, and ways of living
3. an imaginary being with magical powers
4. the main male character in a story, poem, or play

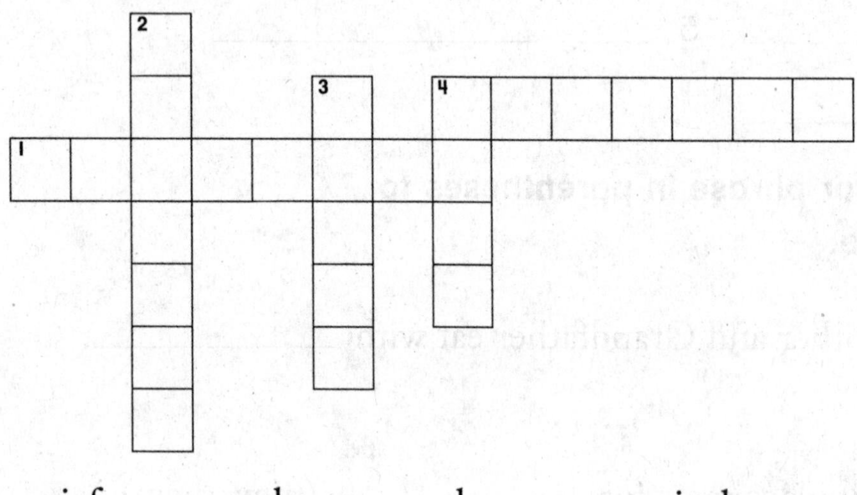

ryiaf ______ reoh ______ rtleuuc ______ inrhoee ______ llkeaoft ______

Name ______________________________

Fairy Tale Chart

	"Cinderella"	"Yeh-Shen"
Characters		
Setting (time and place)		
Problem		
Events *Beginning*	1. Before the ball	1. Before the festival
Middle	2. At the ball, first night	2. At the festival
	3. At the ball, second night	3. After the festival
End	4. Ending	4. Ending

Name ___________________________

Identify Fairy Tale Elements

Complete the chart by adding the missing information.

Who is the main human character?	**Cinderella**	**Yeh-Shen**
How do you know when the story takes place?		
Who or what is the fairy or make-believe character?		
What good fortune does the make-believe character bring?		
What is the happy ending?		

Name ______________________________

Make Up a Fairy Tale!

Read through the story below. Each time you are given a choice of words, circle the one that is a fairy tale element.

1. Last Monday, at 1:00 in the afternoon, / Many years ago a very unusual thing happened. 2. A poor young man from the countryside / A turtle was walking around the streets of a busy town. He heard people talking excitedly about the celebration planned for the palace that night. "I would love to go," he said out loud, "but I don't have anything to wear." 3. A shoemaker / A fairy overheard him. Taking pity, she dressed him in fine clothes. Then she turned the ragged shoes he was wearing into a pair of shiny, bright blue boots. "With these," she said, "you'll be the hit of the party."

That night, as he entered the palace, the princess happened to walk by. She looked down at his boots.

"Nice shoes," she said. "Will you marry me?" They lived happily ever after.

4. ____
"What ugly shoes!" she shouted. The guards threw him out. He cried all the way home.

Name ______________________________

Compare Stories

Complete the diagram with details from the stories.

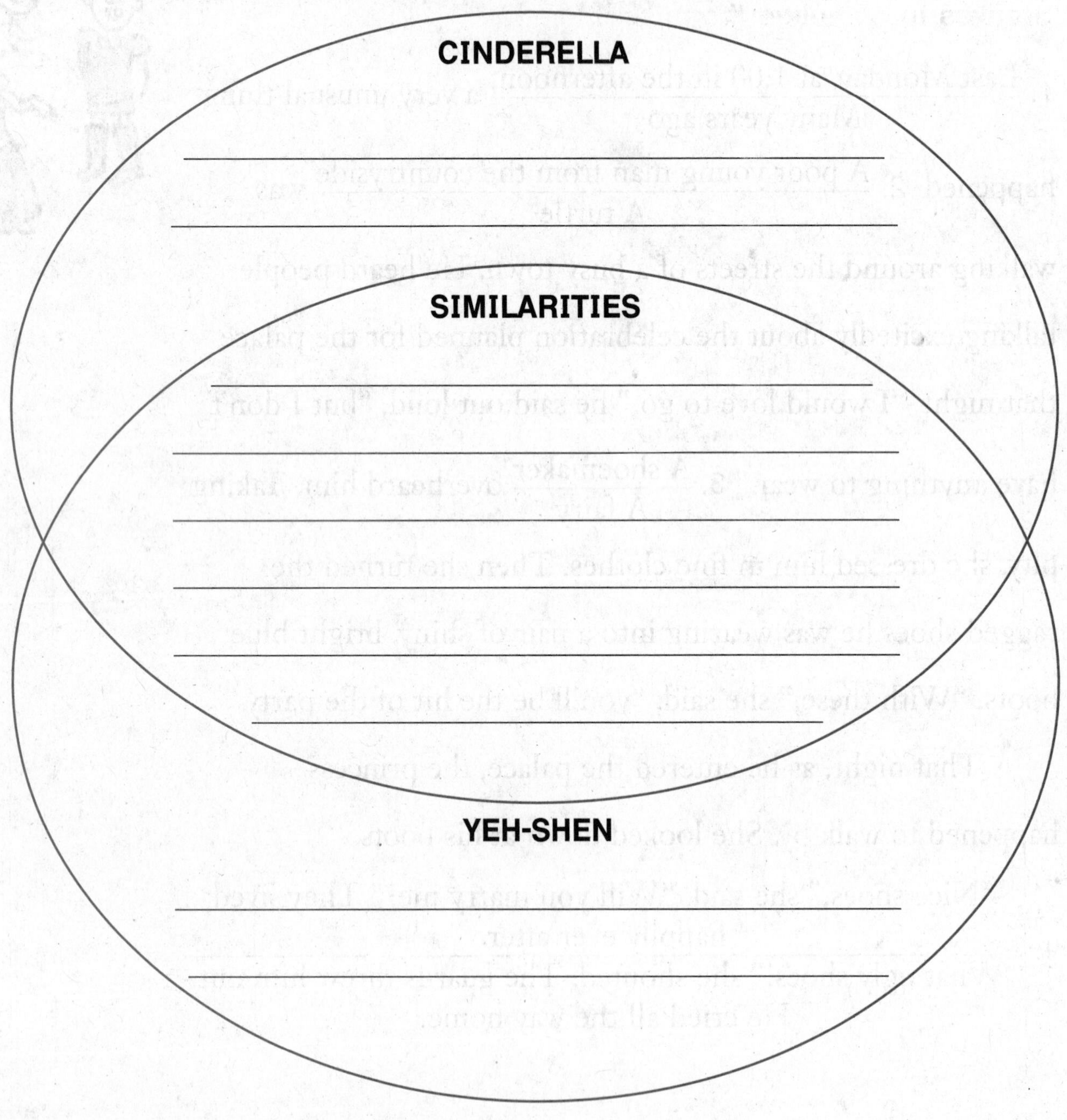

Focus on Fairy Tales

Structural Analysis Prefixes *un-, dis-, re-, non-*; Suffixes *-y, -ly, -ful, -er, -less,* and *-ness*

Name ______________________________

More Prefixes and Suffixes

Write the word that matches each clue in the puzzle. Use the Word Bank and what you know about suffixes and prefixes to complete the puzzle.

Word Bank

retell	fuller	tasteless	unspoken	chilly
neatly	nondairy	softness	truthful	disappear

Across

1. not made of milk
3. not said
6. full of truth
7. more full than
9. quality of being not hard or firm

Down

2. go away without a trace
4. in a tidy way
5. cold
6. not having any taste
8. say again

Focus on Fairy Tales

Spelling Skill Spelling the /s/ Sound in *face*

Name ___________________________

The /s/ Sound in *face*

The /s/ sound may be spelled *c* when the *c* is followed by *e* or *i*.

/s/ fa**ce**, **ci**rcle

Write each Spelling Word under the heading that shows the spelling of the /s/ sound.

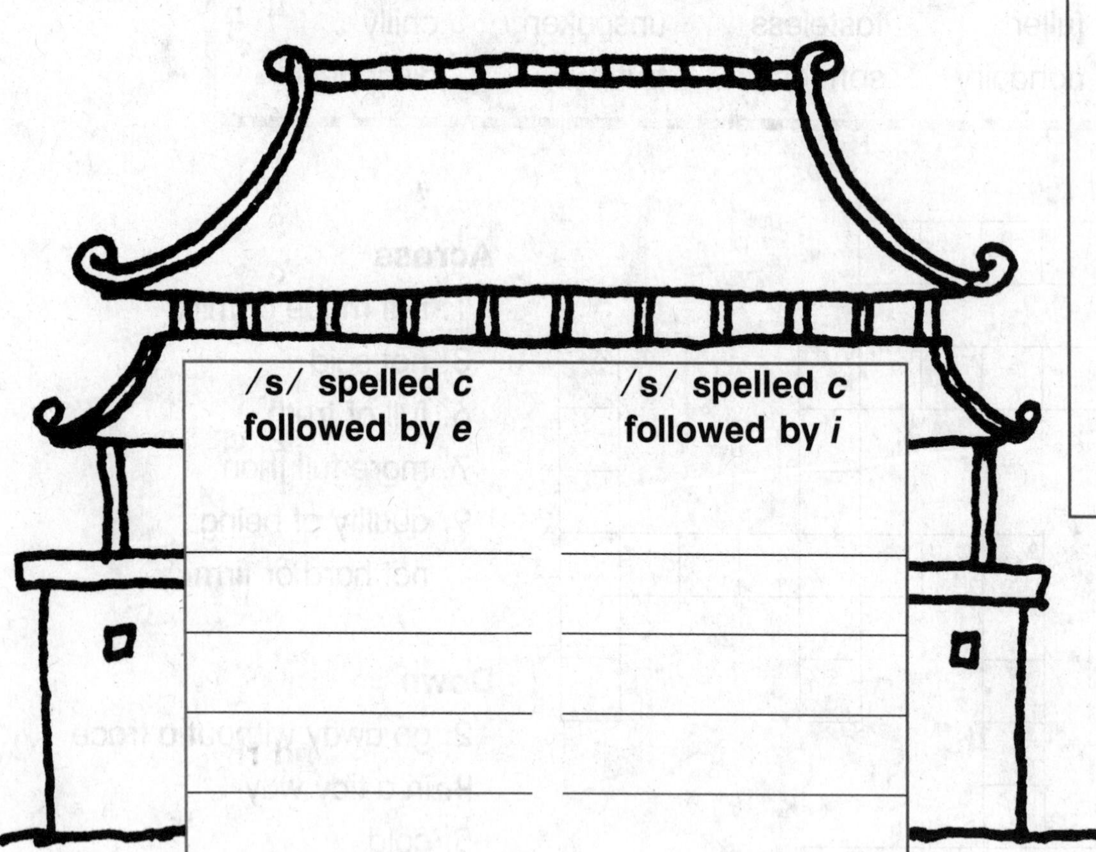

/s/ spelled *c* followed by *e*	/s/ spelled *c* followed by *i*

Spelling Words

1. face
2. city
3. pencil
4. place
5. center
6. dance
7. race
8. circle
9. nice
10. once
11. princess
12. circus

Name ______________________________

Spelling Spree

Picture Clues **Write the Spelling Word that matches each picture.**

1. ______________ 2. ______________ 3. ______________

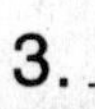

4. ______________ 5. ______________ 6. ______________

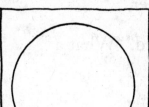

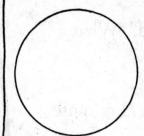

Spelling Words

1. face
2. city
3. pencil
4. place
5. center
6. dance
7. race
8. circle
9. nice
10. once
11. princess
12. circus

Spell and Tell **Write the Spelling Word that fits each clue and rhymes with the word in dark print.**

7. Friendly little cheese-eating animals ______________ **mice**
8. Somewhere that astronauts can go **space** ______________
9. A young cat that lives in a big town ______________ **kitty**
10. A contest in which people try to draw around their hands

    trace ______________

Name ______________________________

Proofreading and Writing

Proofreading Circle the four misspelled Spelling Words in the paragraphs below. Then write each word correctly.

Spelling Words

1. face
2. city
3. pencil
4. place
5. center
6. dance
7. race
8. circle
9. nice
10. once
11. princess
12. circus

There was onse a princess who lived at the top of a tower. One morning a colorful bird flew in her window and landed in the senter of her room. It looked around and then began to danse, hopping from one foot to the other.

The princess was very surprised. "What a strange bird!" she said.

"I'm not strange," said the bird. "I'm quite talented, and I've just escaped from a sercus. Please help me!"

1. ______________ 3. ______________

2. ______________ 4. ______________

Write a TV News Report Think of a fairy tale you know. How would a TV reporter describe the events in the fairy tale to people watching at home?

On a separate sheet of paper, write a short TV report about the main events in the fairy tale. Use Spelling Words from the list.

Name ______________________________

Word Play

Replace the underlined word in each numbered sentence with one word that has a positive connotation and one word that has a negative connotation. Write the connotations on the line below each sentence. Choose your connotations from the Word Bank.

Word Bank

skinny	gazed	slender	curious
weird	guide	pull	glared

Connotation Connection

1. The people at the ball looked at Cinderella.

____

2. The king's son arrived to take her through the crowd.

____

3. The stepsisters' feet were not narrow enough to fit the slipper.

____

4. The people thought it was odd that they had never seen the princess.

____

Name ______________________________

Replacing Nouns with Pronouns

These sentences repeat the same nouns too often. Choose the correct pronoun to replace the underlined word or phrase. Then rewrite each sentence with the pronoun.

1. Yeh-Shen was a lonely orphan, but Yeh-Shen had a pet fish for a friend.

   ____

   ____

2. Yeh-Shen had caught and raised the fish, and the fish lived in a nearby pond.

   ____

   ____

3. Yeh-Shen got some food and shared the food with the fish.

   ____

4. Yeh-Shen asked the old man who the old man was.

   ____

5. The old man disappeared before Yeh-Shen could ask the old man another question.

   ____

   ____

6. The king saw Yeh-Shen take the slipper, and he followed Yeh-Shen home.

   ____

   ____

Focus on Fairy Tales

Grammar Skill Using Pronouns

Name ______________________________

Clear References

Each sentence contains an unclear pronoun. Underline each confusing pronoun. Then rewrite the sentence to make the meaning clear.

Example: Cinderella's stepmother told the family that she would clean the house.

Cinderella's stepmother told the family that Cinderella would clean the house.

1. The sisters asked their parents if they were invited to the ball.

____

____

2. Cinderella's godmother promised that she would attend the ball.

____

____

3. Cinderella asked her godmother when she could help.

____

____

4. The prince told the courier that he would marry the owner of the slipper.

____

____

5. The courier told the prince that he must meet Cinderella.

____

____

Name ______________________________

Correct Pronouns

Use proofreading marks to correct the ten errors in capitalization, end punctuation, and pronoun usage in this short essay about Yeh-Shen and Cinderella.

Example: yeh-Shen lost both of she parents, but Cinderella's father was still alive

Proofreading Marks

- Indent
- Add
- Delete
- Capital letter
- Small letter
- Add Period
- Add Comma
- Add Quotes
- Transpose

Cinderella and Yeh-Shen were very much alike Them both lived with they stepmothers. yeh-Shen had one stepsister, and Cinderella had two? Neither stepmother liked hers stepdaughter. both Cinderella and Yeh-Shen went to a ball. They each lost a slipper, and them ran home. A prince asked Cinderella to marry he. Yeh-Shen married a king

Name ______________________________

Write a Fairy Tale!

Fairy Tale Chart: Your Own Cinderella Tale

Human characters	
Make-believe characters and their powers	
Setting (time and place)	
Problem	
Plot Events	
Beginning	
Middle	
Ending	

Focus on Fairy Tales

Writing Skill Improving Your Writing

Name ______________________________

Adding Similes

Read the paragraph. Fill in each blank to create a simile. Write the answers on the lines below.

At the ball, lights shone as brightly as (1) ________. The music flowed like (2) ________. As the dancers moved across the floor, they twirled like (3) ________. A long table was piled with food, and a bowl of punch as big as a (4) ________ sparkled at one end of the table. The prince sat on his throne, and Cinderella sat near him. They looked as contented as (5) ________ as they enjoyed the evening.

1. ______________________________
2. ______________________________
3. ______________________________
4. ______________________________
5. ______________________________

Name ______________________________

Smart Solutions

Describe a problem that you would like to solve. Tell why you think it is important to solve it.

What could you do to help solve this problem?

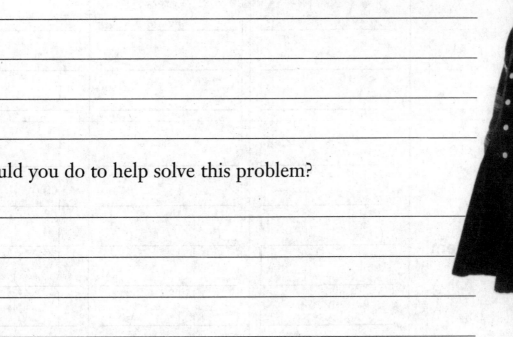

Name ______________________________

Smart Solutions

Fill in the chart as you read the stories.

	Pepita Talks Twice	Poppa's New Pants	Ramona Quimby, Age 8
What is the problem?			
How is the problem solved?			

Name ______________________________

Create a Crossword!

Use the words in the box to create your own crossword puzzle. On another sheet of paper, write a clue for each word you use.

Vocabulary

enchiladas	language	Spanish	salsa
tacos	tamales	tortilla	

Name ___________________________

Problem-Solving Chart

Problem: Pepita does not like having to talk twice.

Possible Solutions	Pros (+) and Cons (–)
1. Stop speaking Spanish.	(+) You wouldn't have to talk twice for people anymore. (–) ______
2. Stop speaking English.	(+) ______ (–) ______
3. Get mad and point out that you don't have time to speak twice.	(+) ______ (–) ______
4. Politely say that you can't speak twice when you don't have time.	(+) ______ (+) ______

Name ______________________________

What Happened?

Mark a T if the sentence is true and an F if it is false. If the sentence is false, rewrite it to make it correct.

1. Pepita's dog is a wolf.

____

2. Some adults in Pepita's neighborhood speak only Spanish.

____

3. Pepita loses her temper when Juan gets home first and teaches Lobo to fetch a ball.

____

4. Before she makes her decision, Pepita thinks about all the problems she might have if she stops speaking Spanish.

____

5. Lobo does not understand Pepita when she speaks in English.

____

6. Pepita's father is happy when he learns that Pepita has stopped speaking Spanish.

____

Write a complete sentence to answer the question below.

What event finally convinces Pepita that it is a good thing to speak both English and Spanish?

____

Name ______________________________

A Homework Problem

Read the story. Then complete the chart on the next page.

The Volcano or Numberland

"Pakki! Help me in the kitchen! Now! Hurry!" I ran down to the kitchen, terrified. There sat my sister, Kayla, drinking milk and calmly reading the television listings in the newspaper.

"What's wrong?" I asked, out of breath from running to the kitchen.

"The science project I've been working on for two weeks is due tomorrow. Ms. Odenpak may give me a bad grade if I don't have my model volcano finished. But a TV show called *Niles in Numberland* is starting in twenty minutes. My math teacher, Mr. Browning, told us to watch it and be ready to talk about it tomorrow in class. What I should do? Help!"

"I have three ideas," I answered. "One, you finish your volcano while I watch the TV show and take notes. Of course, I'm not very good at taking notes," I reminded her. "Two, you can watch the TV show and ask Ms. Odenpak for an extra day to finish your volcano. Or three, you can work on your volcano in front of the television while you take notes on the show."

"Hmm," Kayla answered, thinking deeply. "Which one's the best solution?"

Name ______________________________

A Homework Problem continued

Read the problem. Write one possible solution from the story in each box. Then give a pro and a con about the solution.

The Problem: Kayla needs to finish her science project, and she also needs to watch TV for a math assignment.

Possible Solution: ______________________________

____

Pro: ______________________________

Con: ______________________________

Possible Solution: ______________________________

____

Pro: ______________________________

Con: ______________________________

Possible Solution: ______________________________

____

Pro: ______________________________

Con: ______________________________

Which of these solutions do you think is the best? Why?

____

Name ______________________________

Playing with the Pattern

Read each word in dark type. Then follow the directions to make a new word. Write the new word on the line, and draw a picture in the box to show its meaning.

Example: single Replace **si** with **ju**.

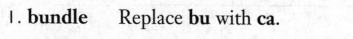

The new word is jungle.

1. **bundle** Replace **bu** with **ca**.

   The new word is ______________.

2. **dollar** Replace **lar** with **phin**.

   The new word is ______________.

3. **twinkle** Replace **twi** with **a**.

   The new word is ______________.

4. **letter** Replace **let** with **mons**.

   The new word is ______________.

5. **turtle** Replace **tur** with **cas**.

   The new word is ______________.

Name ________________________________

Words That End with *er* or *le*

Spelling Words

1. summer
2. winter
3. little
4. October
5. travel*
6. color*
7. apple
8. able
9. November
10. ever
11. later
12. purple

Remember that, in words with more than one syllable, the final /ər/ sounds are often spelled *er*, and the final /əl/ sounds can be spelled *le*.

/ər/ summ**er** /əl/ litt**le**

► In the starred word *travel*, the /əl/ sound is spelled *el*.

► In the starred word *color*, the /ər/ sound is spelled *or*.

Write each Spelling Word under the heading that describes the word.

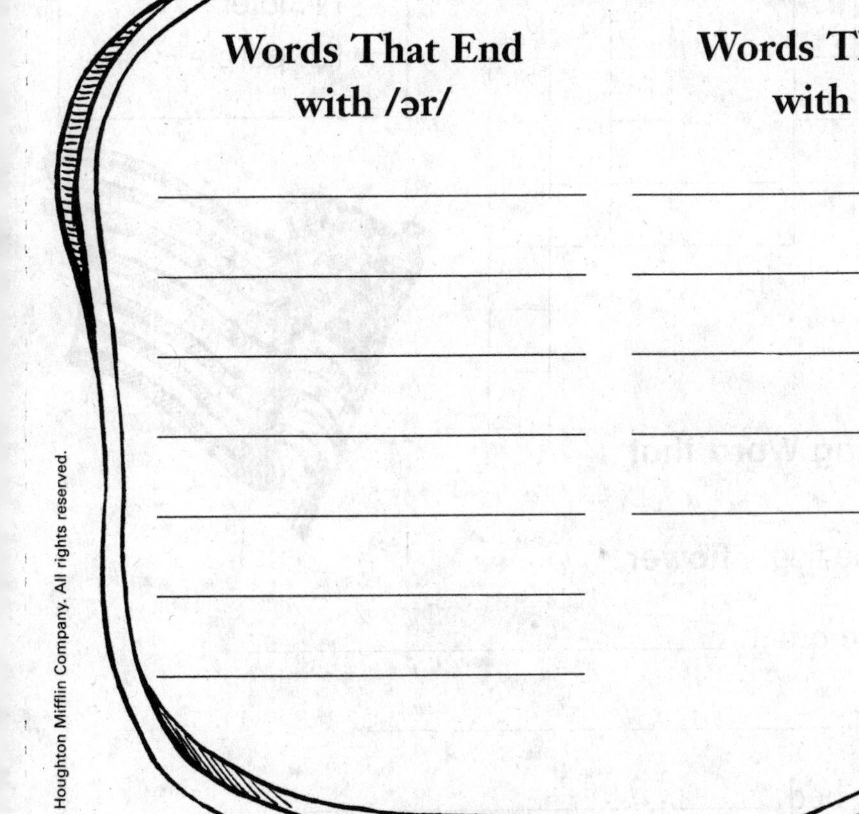

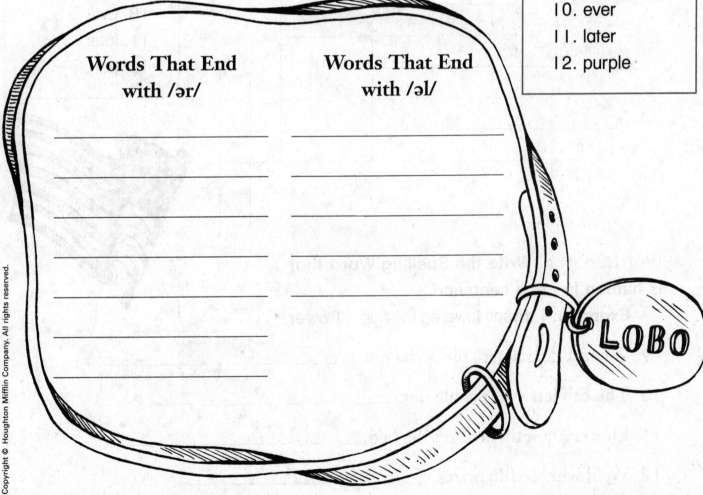

Words That End with /ər/	Words That End with /əl/
____________	____________
____________	____________
____________	____________
____________	____________
____________	____________
____________	
____________	

Name ______________________________

Spelling Spree

Crossword Puzzle Write a Spelling Word in the puzzle that means the same as each clue.

Spelling Words

1. summer
2. winter
3. little
4. October
5. travel*
6. color*
7. apple
8. able
9. November
10. ever
11. later
12. purple

Across

3. the month before December
4. not big
6. the month after September
7. red or yellow or green

Down

1. the hottest season
2. take a trip
4. the opposite of *sooner*
5. a mix of blue and red

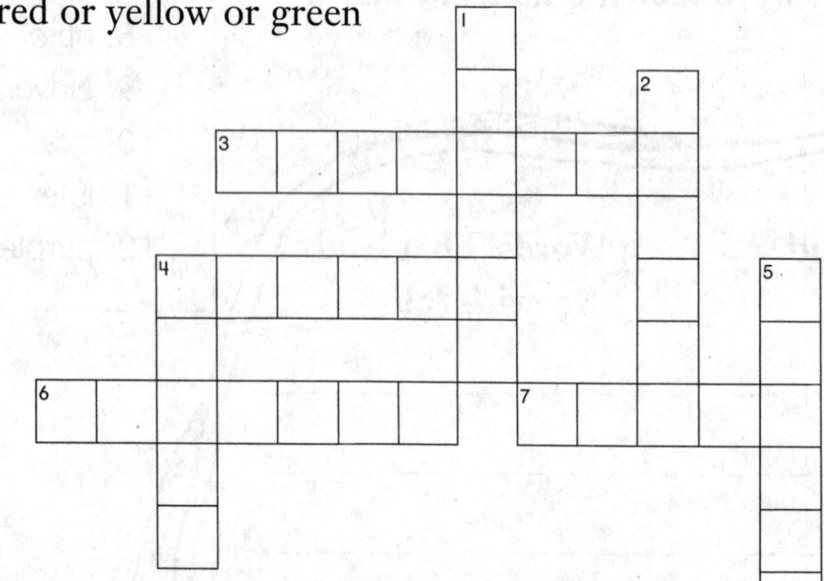

Word Search Write the Spelling Word that is hidden in each sentence.

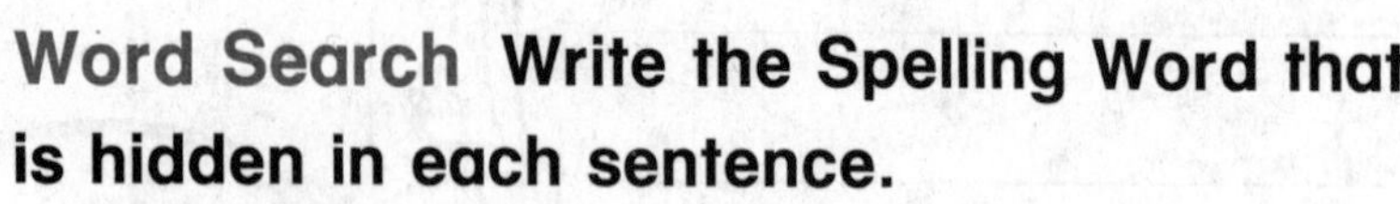

Example: I myself lowered the flag. **flower**

9. When I take a nap, please be quiet. ______________

10. The cab lets two people out. ______________

11. Lie very quietly here on the bed. ______________

12. We'll win terrific prizes! ______________

Name ____________________

Proofreading and Writing

Proofreading Circle the five misspelled Spelling Words in this paragraph. Then write each word correctly.

Sarah liked summir. It was her favorite time of year. The heat did not evir bother her. Her parents, however, did not like the heat. They often wished to travil someplace cool. When Sarah got hot, she rested in the cool kitchen. Later, she would eat a nice, juicy appel. She liked the fruit's pleasant red coler and smooth skin. It was too bad her parents weren't able to enjoy this season as much as she did.

Spelling Words

1. summer
2. winter
3. little
4. October
5. travel*
6. color*
7. apple
8. able
9. November
10. ever
11. later
12. purple

1. ____________________ 4. ____________________

2. ____________________ 5. ____________________

3. ____________________

Write a Paragraph What can Sarah do to help her parents stay cool? How can Sarah get her parents to like the summer as much as she does?

On a separate sheet of paper, write a paragraph about what Sarah might do or say to her parents to help them enjoy the summer. Use Spelling Words from the list.

Name ______________________________

In Other Words

Choose a synonym for each word from the word box below. Write the synonym in the blanks next to the word. Then write each numbered letter in the matching blanks to solve the puzzle.

Word Bank

foolish	loud	stroll	tugged	yell
frighten	speed	tired	wealth	

1. walk ___ ___ ___ ___ ___ ___ (1 under the 2nd blank)
2. shout ___ ___ ___ ___ (3 under the 2nd blank)
3. pulled ___ ___ ___ ___ ___ ___ (6 under the 2nd blank)
4. scare ___ ___ ___ ___ ___ ___ ___ ___ (2 under the 5th blank)
5. sleepy ___ ___ ___ ___ ___ (7 under the 3rd blank)
6. race ___ ___ ___ ___ ___ (4 under the 1st blank)
7. riches ___ ___ ___ ___ ___ ___ (5 under the 3rd blank)
8. noisy ___ ___ ___ ___ (8 under the 3rd blank)
9. silly ___ ___ ___ ___ ___ ___ ___ (9 under the 6th blank)

This is a word for a book of synonyms:

___ ___ ___ ___ ___ ___ ___ ___ ___
1 2 3 4 5 6 7 8 9

Name ______________________

Writing with Adjectives

On the lines to the right of each sentence, list the adjectives. Then write each adjective in the chart below.

1. Pepita has one playful dog. ______________
2. She has many friendly neighbors. ______________
3. Pepita has an unusual problem. ______________
4. She speaks perfect Spanish and English. ______________
5. She does not confuse the two languages. ______________
6. Pepita gets an angry feeling. ______________
7. Juan teaches Lobo a new trick. ______________
8. Mother makes a dozen tacos. ______________
9. She also prepares some salsa. ______________
10. Pepita learns an important lesson. ______________

What Kind?	How Many?	Articles
______	______	______
______	______	______
______	______	______
______	______	
______	______	
______		
______		

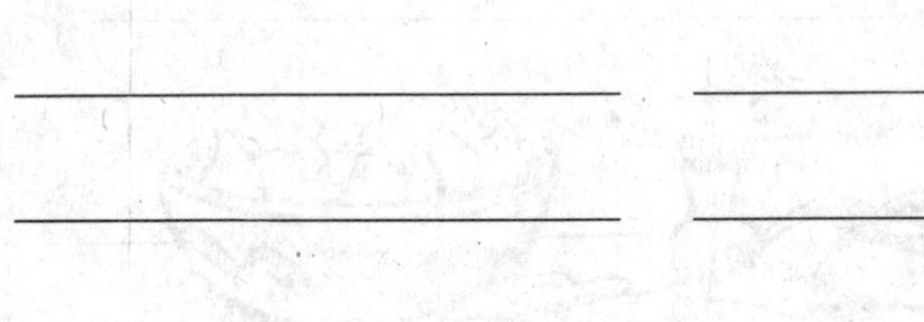

Name ______________________

Adjectives in Paragraphs

Read this paragraph about a neighborhood. Choose an adjective from the box to complete each sentence. Use the clues in parentheses to help you.

Word Bank

an	beautiful	exciting	favorite	full
happy	hundred	long	several	the

Carlos's neighborhood has an ______________ (what kind) block party. Almost a ______________ (how many) people are there. Many people help to prepare ______________(article) excellent meal. Two ______________ (what kind) tables are covered with ______________ (what kind) plates. Carlos and ______________ (how many) neighbors sing their ______________ (what kind) songs. The ______________ (what kind) words are in Spanish. Soon, everyone joins ______________ (article) singers. Even the dog woofs a ______________ (what kind) bark at the end of every song.

Name ______________________________

Expanding Sentences with Adjectives

Rewrite each sentence. Add at least one adjective to each sentence. Remember that you may need to change *a* or *an*, too.

1. Pepita and Juan have a dog.

____

2. Pepita goes to a picnic.

____

3. She helps prepare the food.

____

4. The neighbors sing songs.

____

5. Lobo almost runs into a truck.

____

6. Pepita calls the dog.

____

7. The dog hears her shout.

____

8. She gives Lobo a hug.

____

Name ______________________________

Announcement Planner

Use this page to organize your ideas for an announcement. Write an announcement about a birth, wedding, concert, fair, parade, or other special event.

Who?	What?	Where?	When?	Why?	How?

ANNOUNCEMENT

____

____

____

____

____

____

____

Name ______________________________

Ordering Important Information

- When writing an announcement, first decide what information is most important. Put that information first.
- Put other information in order of importance from most important to least important.
- Be sure your announcement includes all the necessary information that answers some or all of these questions: Who? What? Where? When? How? Why?

Number the information in the order it should go in the announcement. Write 1 for the first thing that should be in the announcement. Write 2 for the second thing.

_____ Practice will be at Jamal's house.

_____ Practice will end at noon.

_____ There will be band practice on Saturday.

_____ Practice begins at 10:00 a.m.

_____ Jamal's address is 32 Windsor Lane.

Rewrite the announcement in the order you marked.

____

____

____

____

____

____

Name ___________________________

Revising Your Persuasive Essay

Reread your essay. Put a checkmark in the box for each sentence that describes your paper. Use this page to help you revise.

Rings the Bell

- ☐ My essay focuses on a goal supported by reasons.
- ☐ Each reason is supported by facts and examples.
- ☐ I told my goal in the beginning. I retold it in the end.
- ☐ I used persuasive words that show how I feel.
- ☐ My sentences flow well. There are few mistakes.

Getting Stronger

- ☐ The essay could be more focused. I need more reasons.
- ☐ There could be more facts and examples.
- ☐ I forgot to write a beginning or an ending.
- ☐ I need more persuasive words. It's not clear how I feel.
- ☐ Some sentences are choppy. There are some mistakes.

Try Harder

- ☐ The goal is not clear. There are almost no reasons.
- ☐ There are no facts or examples.
- ☐ Both the beginning and the ending are missing.
- ☐ I used no persuasive words. I don't seem to care.
- ☐ Most sentences are choppy. There are many mistakes.

Name ____________________

Correcting Run-On Sentences

Fix these run-on sentences. Write the sentences correctly on the lines provided.

1. Run-On: Jane Goodall is one of the world's great scientists, she studies chimpanzees.

   Corrected: ____________________

2. Run-On: More than thirty years ago Goodall had an interesting idea, she would study chimps in their natural habitat.

   Corrected: ____________________

3. Run-On: At first, the chimps were suspicious, gradually Goodall gained their trust.

   Corrected: ____________________

4. Run-On: Goodall got to know each chimp in the group, each chimp was given a name.

   Corrected: ____________________

5. Run-On: Goodall was the first to discover that chimps made tools, she also discovered that chimps could learn new ideas.

   Corrected: ____________________

Reading-Writing Workshop

Frequently Misspelled Words

Name ______________________________

Spelling Words

Look for spelling patterns you have learned to help you remember the Spelling Words on this page. Think about the parts that you find hard to spell.

Write the missing letters and apostrophes in the Spelling Words below.

1. h _____ _____
2. I _____ _____
3. I _____ _____
4. th _____ _____ _____ _____
5. did _____ _____ _____
6. do _____ _____ _____
7. _____ _____ ow
8. _____ _____ tsid _____
9. b _____ _____ n
10. we _____ _____ _____
11. _____ nyone
12. _____ nyway

Spelling Words

1. his
2. I'd
3. I'm
4. that's
5. didn't
6. don't
7. know
8. outside
9. been
10. we're
11. anyone
12. anyway

Study List On another sheet of paper, write each Spelling Word. Check the list to be sure you spelled each word correctly.

Name ____________________

Spelling Spree

Contraction Math Add the first word to the second word to get a contraction from the Spelling Word list.

1. do + not = _____
2. we + are = _____
3. that + is = _____
4. I + had = _____
5. did + not = _____
6. I + am = _____

1. ____________________
2. ____________________
3. ____________________
4. ____________________
5. ____________________
6. ____________________

Spelling Words

1. his
2. I'd
3. I'm
4. that's
5. didn't
6. don't
7. know
8. outside
9. been
10. we're
11. anyone
12. anyway

Fill in the Blanks Fill each blank in these sentences with the Spelling Word that makes the most sense.

It's freezing __7__! Has __8__ seen my jacket? I've __9__ keeping it on the floor in my room, but it's not there. Now I don't __10__ where it is. Dad said it's not in __11__ study, either. Well __12__, if you see it, let me know.

7. ____________________
8. ____________________
9. ____________________
10. ____________________
11. ____________________
12. ____________________

Name ____________________

Proofreading and Writing

Proofreading **Circle the four misspelled Spelling Words in this advertisement. Then write each word correctly.**

Do you have a problem that you don't kno how to solve? Then call us at Smart Solutions! We've bin solving people's problems for over twenty years. And anywon will tell you that our prices can't be beat. So give us a call at 555-1971 — weare waiting!

Spelling Words

1. his
2. I'd
3. I'm
4. that's
5. didn't
6. don't
7. know
8. outside
9. been
10. we're
11. anyone
12. anyway

1. ____________ 3. ____________

2. ____________ 4. ____________

Write a Caption **Draw a picture of a problem that needs to be solved. Then write a caption describing the problem and how to fix it. Use Spelling Words from the list.**

Name ____________________

Sewing Words

Fill in the blanks with the correct word from the Word Bank. (Hint: Not every word will be used.) Then find and circle all the Word Bank words in the puzzle.

Word Bank

fabric	hem	mended	pattern
rustling	plaid	draped	

1. Another word for cloth is ____________________.
2. To make pants shorter, you could ______________ them.
3. A shirt with a hole in it needs to be ____________________.
4. Different-colored stripes that cross one another make a design called ____________________.
5. If you are wearing a shirt with a decorative design on it, the shirt has a ____________________.

C R R D R A P E D M Q Y S
F L U B F D A S O G M R E
O T S N A C T T M J P E D
H Q T U B B T Y E G L U C
E M L N R J E M N Y A A A
M C I W I J R P D N I S O
Z U N V C H N S E O D S Z
K E G B Q T W G D W U O I
H E Q E B Y Q J E F P R J

Name ______________________________

Conclusions Chart

Pages	Questions
284–286	1. What is the narrator's name? ____________ Which story clues helped you? ____________ ____________
286	2. How does Poppa feel about plaid pants? ____________ Which story clues helped you? ____________ ____________
288	3. How does George feel about being kissed by Big Mama and Aunt Viney? ____________ Which story clues helped you? ____________ ____________
292	4. Who is the first shape? ____________ Which story clues helped you? ____________

Poppa's New Pants

Comprehension Check

Name ______________________

Who, What, and Why?

Use complete sentences to answer the questions about *Poppa's New Pants.*

Who comes to visit Grandma Tiny, Poppa, and George?

____

What is wrong with the pants Poppa buys?

____

Why won't the women hem Poppa's pants?

____

Why does George have trouble getting to sleep?

____

____

What weird sights does George see?

____

____

What is Grandma Tiny's surprise?

____

Why do the women surprise each other?

____

____

Why does George feel lucky about the mix-up?

____

____

Name ______________________________

Drawing Conclusions

Read the story. Then complete the chart on the next page.

The Pink Sweatshirt

"But Mom, I need a *pink* sweatshirt for our play!" I argued. "I'm the pig who builds with bricks! We need pink sweatshirts with hoods so we can sew on pink felt ears."

"Linda, I just bought you a white sweatshirt," said Mom. "You'll have to spend your own money if you want a pink one."

I was saving all my money for a new bike. "Oh, Mom! Tina's and Ali's parents are buying them pink ones," I whined.

This did not convince my mother. "Lots of pigs aren't pink," she said firmly. "You can be a white pig in a white sweatshirt."

But Tina, Ali, and I wanted our costumes to match. So, I got my new pair of red shorts, the ones labeled, "Wash in COLD WATER only." I dumped those and my white sweatshirt into the washing machine. Then I punched the button marked HOT WATER. Too bad I didn't look in the washer first! The load of white laundry left in there got washed again (in hot water) with my sweatshirt and red shorts.

So, today I'm spending my savings on new white socks for my brother, a white shirt for Dad, and four white towels. Luckily, Dad likes the new color of his bathrobe. It reminds him of a strawberry milkshake.

Name ______________________________

Drawing Conclusions continued

Answer each question about "The Pink Sweatshirt." Then tell which story clues helped you to draw that conclusion.

1. Who is the girl telling the story?

____

Story Clues: ______________________________

____

2. What happens when you wash red and white laundry together in hot water?

____

Story Clues: ______________________________

____

____

3. What other laundry was already in the washing machine?

____

Story Clues: ______________________________

____

4. Why must Linda spend the money she is trying to save?

____

Story Clues: ______________________________

____

Name ______________________________

Which One Belongs?

Write the word from the box that belongs in each group.

Word Bank

cover	writer	below	finish	second
siren	female	frozen	shiver	clever

1. instant, moment, ____________________
2. under, beneath, ____________________
3. shake, tremble, ____________________
4. cold, icy, ____________________
5. smart, intelligent, ____________________
6. author, poet, ____________________
7. whistle, horn, ____________________
8. hide, cloak, ____________________
9. girl, woman, ____________________
10. end, complete, ____________________

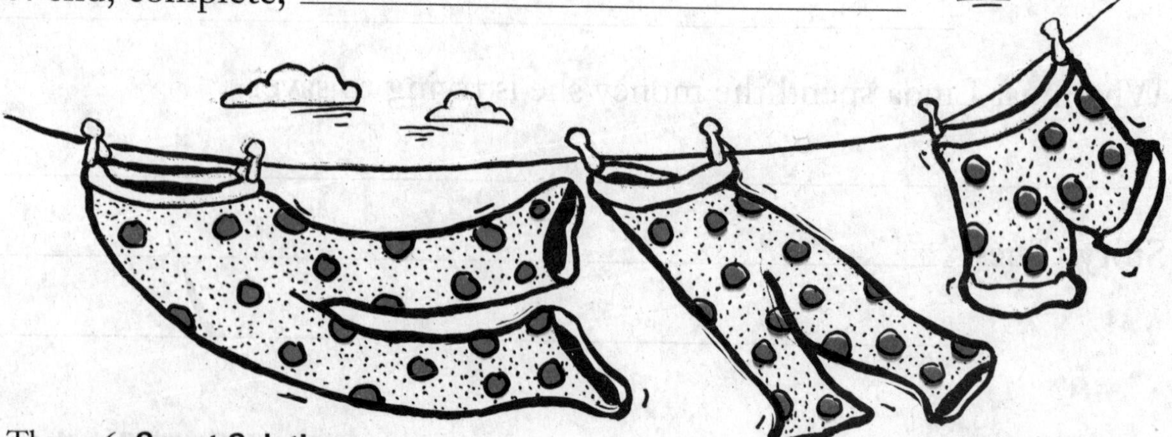

Name ______________________________

Words That Begin with *a* or *be*

In two-syllable words, the unstressed /ə/ sound at the beginning of a word may be spelled *a*. The unstressed /bĭ/ sounds may be spelled *be*.

/ə/ **a**gain /bĭ/ **be**fore

Write each Spelling Word under the heading that tells how the word begins.

Spelling Words

1. began
2. again
3. around
4. before
5. away
6. about
7. alive
8. because
9. ahead
10. between
11. behind
12. ago

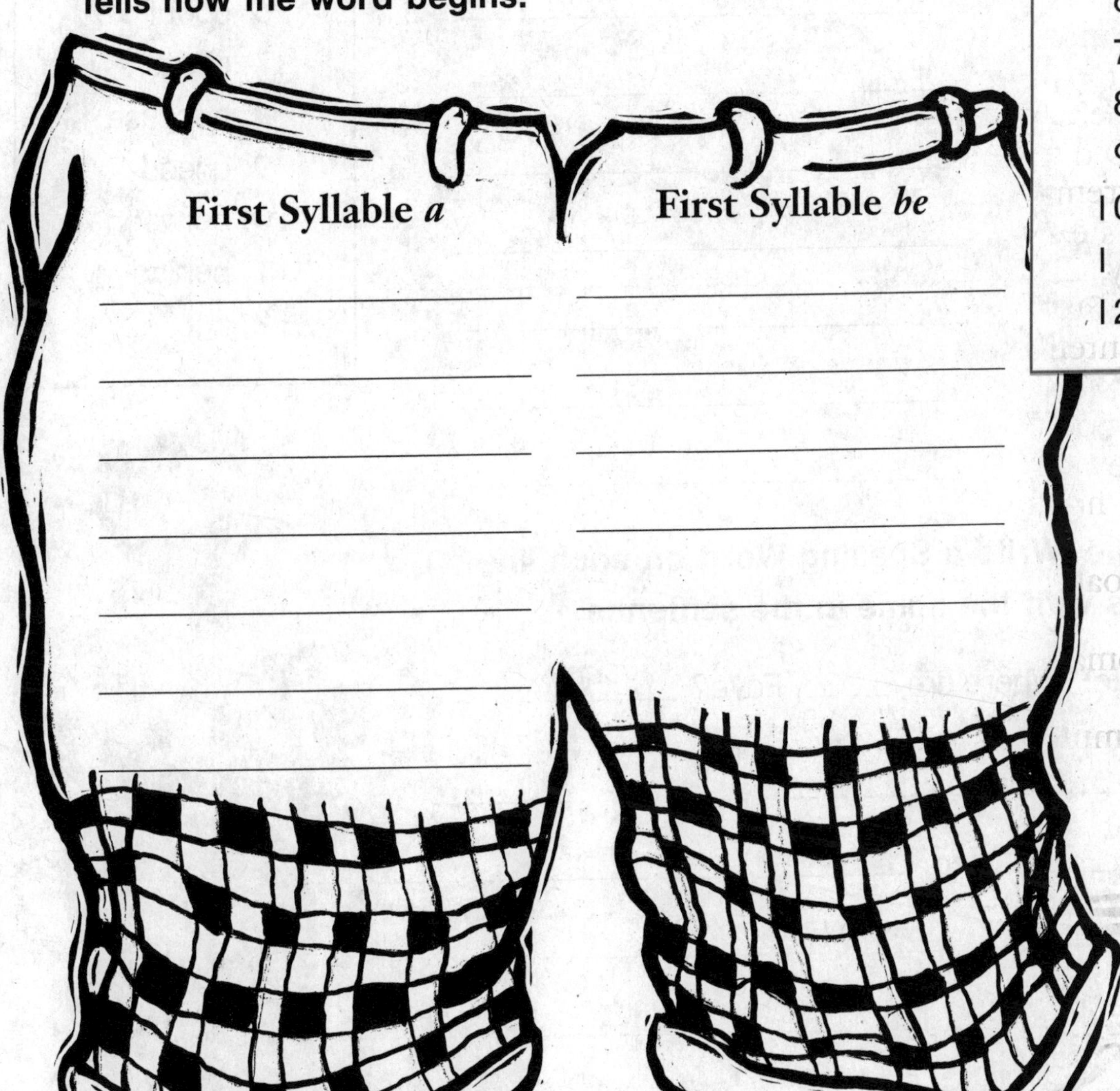

First Syllable *a*	First Syllable *be*
______	______
______	______
______	______
______	______
______	______
______	
______	

Name ______________________

Spelling Spree

Code Breaker **Use the code to figure out each Spelling Word below. Then write the word.**

∞ = be ⊗ = n ^ = a ∇ = i ↵ = g _ = o

Example: ∞ t w e e ⊗ between

1. ^ w ^ y ______
2. ^ b _ u t ______
3. ∞ h ∇ ⊗ d ______
4. ∞ c ^ u s e ______
5. ^ ↵ ^ ∇ ⊗ ______
6. ^ r _ u ⊗ d ______
7. ∞ f _ r e ______

Spelling Words

1. began
2. again
3. around
4. before
5. away
6. about
7. alive
8. because
9. ahead
10. between
11. behind
12. ago

Rhyme Time **Write a Spelling Word on each line that rhymes with the name in the sentence.**

Example: Where are ____, Faye? they

8. It's ____, Clive. ______
9. What's ____, Ned? ______
10. That was long ____, Joe. ______
11. We already ____, Jan. ______
12. Put them in ____, Jean. ______

Name ______________________________

Proofreading and Writing

Proofreading **Circle the five misspelled Spelling Words in this journal entry. Then write each word correctly.**

It all bigan after I brought home my fancy new pants. I couldn't wear them becaus they were too long. No one eround the house could help me make them shorter. Everyone was too tired. Then, bifor morning, the pants were too short! Someone got up in the night to fix them. This happened agin and then again. Now they are just about perfect for my son.

Spelling Words

1. began
2. again
3. around
4. before
5. away
6. about
7. alive
8. because
9. ahead
10. between
11. behind
12. ago

1. ______________________
2. ______________________
3. ______________________
4. ______________________
5. ______________________

Take a Survey Ask two or three friends about what others have done to help them. Take notes.

On a separate sheet of paper, write about how people helped your friends. Use Spelling Words from the list.

Name ______________________________

Antonym Crossword Puzzle

Read each clue. Then choose an antonym from the word bank and fill in the correct boxes on the crossword puzzle. Use a dictionary for help.

Word Bank

dirty
empty
fancy
fast
forget
found
happy
last
tall
thin

Across

2. lost
4. first
6. remember
8. thick

Down

1. slow
3. clean
5. short
6. plain
7. full
9. sad

Name ________________________________

Writing Comparisons

Complete this chart with the correct forms of the adjective.

Adjective	Compare Two Things	Compare More Than Two Things
short	shorter	shortest
loud	1. ________________	2. ________________
soft	3. ________________	4. ________________
bold	5. ________________	6. ________________
quiet	7. ________________	8. ________________
sharp	9. ________________	10. ________________

Choose a word from the chart to complete each sentence.

11. The gray fabric is ________________ than the red fabric.

12. Big Mama is the ________________ ghost.

13. The ________________ sound came right after midnight.

14. Aunt Viney is a ________________ speaker than Grandma Tiny.

15. Big Mama takes the ________________ needle from her sewing kit.

Name ______________________________

Writing the Correct Form

Write the correct form of the adjective in parentheses to complete each sentence.

1. Poppa's new pants are ______________________ than his old pants. (long)
2. Big Mama is ______________________ than her sister. (old)
3. Aunt Viney is the ______________________ sewer of the three ghosts. (fast)
4. The snipping sound is ______________________ than a whisper. (loud)
5. Grandma Tiny is the ______________________ of all. (loud)
6. Poppa is ______________________ than George. (tall)
7. George thinks the second ghost is ______________________ than the first. (odd)
8. Now Poppa's pants are the ______________________ pants in the house. (short)
9. George has ______________________ legs than Poppa. (short)
10. This story is the ______________________ story I know. (weird)

Name ______________________________

A Good Story, Well Told

Using *good* and *well* **Suppose George wrote a letter.Proofread the letter. Check that *good* and *well* are used correctly. Check for spelling errors too. Rewrite the letter below.**

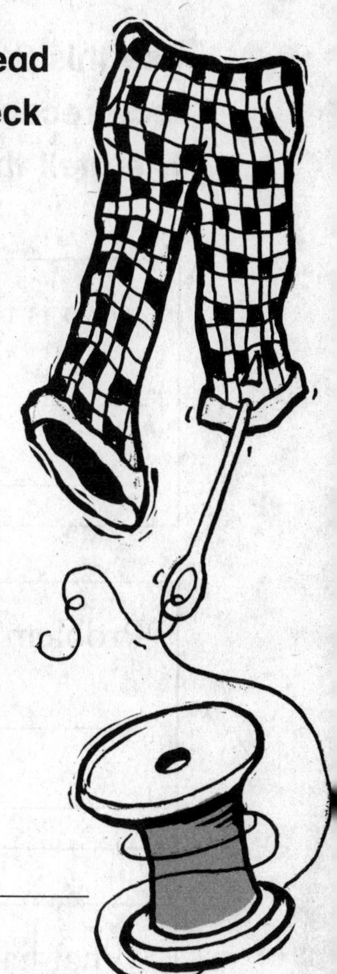

Dear Cousin,

Poppa bought a well new pair of pants last week. But they did not fit him good, so Poppa asked Big Mama, Grandma Tiny, and Aunt Viney to hemm the pants. They said no. Poppa was a little sad, but he is a good man. He didn't complain. Guess what happened next! All three women got up in the middle of the night. They each mennded the pants!

When Poppa woke up, he got a well shock. His new pants had turned into shorts. Luckily, the pants fit me good.

Your cousin,
George

____

____

____

____

____

____

____

____

____

____

Name ________________________

Story Map

Use this Story Map to plan a summary of a story you have read recently. Remember to tell who the story is about. Then tell the main things that happened in the story.

Who is the story about?

____

____

Problem

____

____

What happens?

____

____

How does it end?

____

____

Name ______________________________

Paraphrasing

- Paraphrasing is restating something in your own words, without changing the author's meaning.
- Writers use paraphrasing when they write a summary or notes for a report.

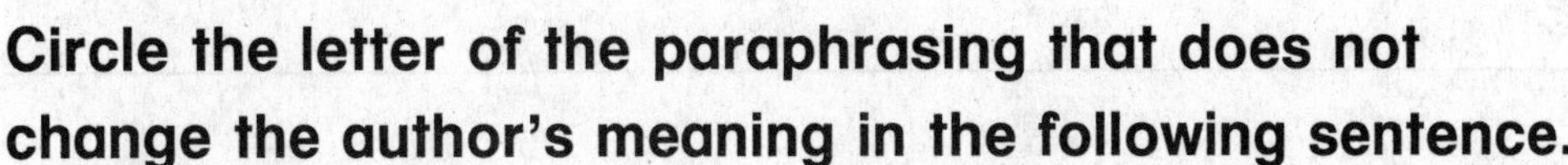

Circle the letter of the paraphrasing that does not change the author's meaning in the following sentence.

"Grandma Tiny's about to bust a gusset making sure everything's just right."

A. "Grandma Tiny is working hard to make sure everything is just right."

B. "Grandma Tiny is working so hard that she broke something."

Paraphrase each sentence:

1. Aunt Viney and Big Mama took turns covering my face with red lipstick.

____

2. Grandma Tiny, Big Mama, and Aunt Viney usually have a good long gossip spell when they get together.

____

____

3. I stayed balled up under those blankets like an armadillo for the rest of the night.

____

4. Grandma Tiny was smiling fit to beat the band.

____

Name ___________________________

A Rainy-Day Survey!

Write sentences to answer the following questions.

1. Do you think rainy days are **dismal** and **dreary**? Why or why not?

 ____

 ____

2. On days when the rain is **ceaseless**, what do you do?

 ____

 ____

3. Do you like the sound of rain **pelting** against your window?

 ____

 ____

4. What do you do when you feel **companionable**?

 ____

 ____

5. What advice would you give to a friend who feels **discouraged**?

 ____

 ____

6. What activity makes you feel **exhausted**?

 ____

 ____

Name ______________________________

Generalizations Chart

Rainy Days	Older Sisters
Parents	**Restaurants**

In general, what statement can you make about people's feelings on rainy days?

____

____

Name ____________________________________

Ramona's Diary

Suppose Ramona kept a diary. Finish this entry with details from *Ramona Quimby, Age 8*.

Dear Diary,

Sunday afternoon was ____________________________________.
Mom and Dad were ____________________________________.
Mom kept reminding me to ____________________________________.
Then Beezus asked Mom to ____________________________________
____________________________________. But Mom and Dad
said no, so Beezus was upset.

Then Dad decided that we should go to the Whopperburger.
He wanted us to ____________________________________.
While we were waiting for our seats, ____________________________________
____________________________________. Dinner was really tasty
and fun too!

Before the man left, he ____________________________________
____________________________________. On the way home, all
of us were ____________________________________.

Name ____________________________________

Making Cafeteria Food

Read the story below. Then answer the questions on the next page.

Ms. Mallard and Meatloaf

Luis dropped his lunch tray on the table next to his friend Joey and sat down. "Can you believe this? They call this meatloaf!" Luis said. "And they just served it two weeks ago! I can't stand it."

"Then why don't you ask someone why it's always on the menu, Luis?" Joey replied. "All you do is complain."

"You're right. I will." Luis stood up and walked directly back to the serving line where the lunch lady was cleaning up. "Um, Ms. Mallard? Can I ask you something?"

Ms. Mallard turned around. "Ah, yes, of course, Luis. What is it? Enjoying your meatloaf?"

"Not really. That's why I'm here. How come you serve it every two weeks and why does it taste so strange?"

"Well, Luis, schools have rules about the kinds of food we serve," Ms. Mallard responded. "We need to make food that fits in the basic food groups. Meatloaf fits most of them, it's easy to make a lot of, and it doesn't cost much to make. That's why many schools put it on their menus."

"Okay, I get it. But how come it tastes so funny?"

"I can tell you, Luis, that you're not alone on this one. Last summer I went to a national meeting about cafeteria food. Almost everybody I talked to said how much the kids dislike the taste of meatloaf. It probably has something to do with the onions and the peppers in it. Not to mention the dry bread that goes in it. Some people just look at its color and think it can't taste good. That's why. Just try putting ketchup on it."

Ramona Quimby, Age 8

Comprehension Skill
Making Generalizations

Name ______________________________

Making Cafeteria Food continued

Answer the following questions based on the story "Ms. Mallard and Meatloaf."

What broad statement can you make about schools and meatloaf?

____

____

What details support your generalization?

____

____

____

____

In general, what can you say about kids and the school meatloaf?

____

____

What details support your generalization?

____

____

____

____

Name ______________________________

Contraction Puzzler

What did Ramona learn on that rainy Sunday? Solve the puzzle to find out. Write the two words that each contraction is made from. Write only one letter on each line. Then write each numbered letter on the line with the matching number below.

1. we're ___ ___ ___(3) ___ ___
2. she's ___ ___ ___(10) ___(13) ___
3. wasn't ___ ___ ___ ___(7) ___ ___
4. you're ___ ___ ___ ___ ___(4) ___
5. he'll ___ ___ ___(1) ___ ___
6. they've ___ ___ ___ ___ ___ ___(11) ___ ___(5)
7. couldn't ___(9) ___ ___ ___(14) ___ ___ ___ ___
8. I'm ___(8) ___ ___(12)
9. they'd ___ ___ ___(2) ___(15) ___ ___ ___ ___ ___
10. aren't ___(6) ___ ___ ___ ___ ___

What Ramona learned:

___(1) ___(2) ___(3) ___(4) ___(5) ___(6) ___(7) ___(8) ___(9) ___(10)

f ___(11) ___(12) ___(13) ___(14) ___(15)

Name ______________________________

Contractions

A contraction is a short way of saying or writing two or more words. An apostrophe takes the place of one or more letters.

I am → **I'm** are not → **aren't**

► The starred words use different patterns.

will not → **won't** of the clock → **o'clock**

Write each Spelling Word under the heading that tells about it.

Spelling Words

1. I'm
2. he's
3. aren't
4. couldn't
5. won't*
6. o'clock*
7. wouldn't
8. weren't
9. she's
10. wasn't
11. I'd
12. shouldn't

Contractions with *not*	Other Contractions
______________	______________
______________	______________
______________	______________
______________	______________
______________	______________
______________	
______________	

Name ______________________

Spelling Spree

Book Titles **Write the Spelling Word that best completes each funny book title. Remember to use capital letters.**

Example: *No Puzzle I ____ or Wouldn't Solve* by I. M. Smarte Couldn't

1. *The Clock Stopped at One* ____ by Minnie T. Hand
2. ____ *You Glad I'm Here?* by Happy A. Ginn
3. ____ *My Brother: A True Story* by N. O. Kidding
4. *The Man Who* ____ *a Spy* by Minny Kluze

1. ______________ 3. ______________

2. ______________ 4. ______________

Spelling Words

1. I'm
2. he's
3. aren't
4. couldn't
5. won't
6. o'clock*
7. wouldn't
8. weren't
9. she's
10. wasn't
11. I'd
12. shouldn't

Make It Shorter **Circle the words below that could be written as contractions. Then write them as contractions on the lines.**

5. Mom would not let you do that.
6. You should not even ask her.
7. She is reading the paper.
8. It was not a good idea.

5. ______________
6. ______________
7. ______________
8. ______________

Name ______________________

Proofreading and Writing

Proofreading Suppose Ramona wrote a note. Circle the five misspelled Spelling Words in the note. Then write each word correctly.

Sunday, 8 o'clock

Dear Mom and Dad,

Id like to thank you for taking us to the Whopperburger. We were'nt having a good day until then. Even Beezus is happier now, but she woen't admit it. Aren't you glad the old man was there? I could'nt believe that he paid for our meal. I'am glad we're a family.

Love,
Ramona

Spelling Words

1. I'm
2. he's
3. aren't
4. couldn't
5. won't*
6. o'clock*
7. wouldn't
8. weren't
9. she's
10. wasn't
11. I'd
12. shouldn't

1. ______________
2. ______________
3. ______________
4. ______________
5. ______________

Write a Skit Choose a scene to act out from *Ramona Quimby, Age 8*, or make up your own scene with two people from her family.

Write the words that the characters might say to each other. Use Spelling Words from the list.

Name ______________________________

Find the Correct Word

Write the missing word in each sentence. A sample word at the end of each sentence gives a clue about the vowel sound. Find the correct word on the word list and write it in the blank. Then circle the letters in the word that match the vowel sound in the sample word. Look at the spelling table for help.

Word Bank

scent
south
dough
foil
hood
heat

1. The furnace will ____________________ the whole house. **beast**
2. Lin put on her gloves and ____________________ in the snowstorm. **good**
3. The ____________________ kept my sandwich fresh. **join**
4. The cook placed the pie ____________________ into a pan. **though**
5. Birds fly ____________________ when the weather gets cold. **house**
6. What is that lovely ____________________ coming from the kitchen? **went**

Spelling Table

/ă/ bat	/ē/ beast	/ŏ/ pond	/ŏŏ/ good
/ā/ play	/ĭ/ give	/ō/ though	/ōō/ house
/â/ care	/ī/ time	/ô/ paw	
/ĕ/ went	/î/ near	/oi/ join	

Name ______________________________

Circling Adverbially

Circle the adverbs in each sentence. Then write the adverbs in the chart below.

1. Ramona watches the rain sadly.
2. Then she looks around in the kitchen.
3. Beezus was crying loudly upstairs.
4. Next, Mrs. Quimby gently scolded Ramona.
5. Nearby, Mr. Quimby read his book silently.
6. Ramona often reads stories to Willa Jean.
7. The pelting rain falls everywhere.
8. "I wanted to bicycle today," she thought sulkily.
9. Finally, Mr. Quimby decided to cheer everyone up.
10. They decided to eat out at Whopperburger.

How	When	Where
______	______	______
______	______	______
______	______	______
______	______	______
______	______	______

Name ______________________________

Choosing Adverbs

Choose an adverb from the box to complete each sentence. Use the clue in parentheses to help you.

Word Bank

around
completely
inside
loudly
often
out
quickly
sharply
slowly
quietly

Mr. Quimby parked the car and the family walked ____________________ (where). The customers filled the restaurant ____________________ (how). Ramona and Beezus quarreled ____________________ (how). Mrs. Quimby scolded them ____________________ (how). When they were seated, they ordered ____________________ (how). Soon the waitress appeared. She carried platters of food ____________________ (where) of the kitchen.

The Quimbys sat at the table ____________________(how). Ramona ate ____________________(how). She wished the meal could last forever. She ____________________ (when) wished for impossible things. Ramona looked ____________________(where). She wanted to remember her perfect meal.

Name ______________________________

Expanding Sentences with Adverbs

Add one adverb to each sentence. In the first five sentences, add the adverb in the blank. Use the clues in parentheses to help you. In the other sentences, decide where to add the adverb.

1. Mother talks ____________________ to Becky. (how)
2. Mother ____________________ talks to Becky. (when)
3. Becky looks ____________________ for Fluffy. (where)
4. "I want to sleep over at Mimi's," Susan shouted ____________________. (how)
5. ____________________ Susan was in tears. (when)
6. Susan slammed her door.

   ____

7. Becky had listened to the quarrel.

   ____

8. She decided to talk to Susan.

   ____

9. "May I come in?" asked Becky.

   ____

10. "Sure," said Susan, "I will only talk to you and our cat."

   ____

Name ______________________________

Planning Your Personal Essay

Use this graphic organizer to help you plan your personal essay. Write your main idea in the top box. Then write two reasons or facts about your idea in the boxes below. Think of details and examples for each reason. Then summarize your main idea in the last box.

My Main Idea:

____

____

Reason 1:

____

____

Reason 2:

____

____

Reason 1 Examples and Details:

____

____

____

Reason 2 Examples and Details:

____

____

____

Summary and restatement of main idea:

____

____

Name ______________________________

Telling More with Adverbs

Adverbs can modify verbs. Good writers use adverbs to tell more about an action. They can tell *how* or *when*.

The cat is meowing.

The cat is meowing **loudly**. (tells *how*)

The cat is meowing **now**. (tells *when*)

Adverbs That Tell How		Adverbs That Tell When	
sadly	patiently	always	tomorrow
silently	secretly	finally	now
loudly	quickly	never	daily
slowly		yesterday	

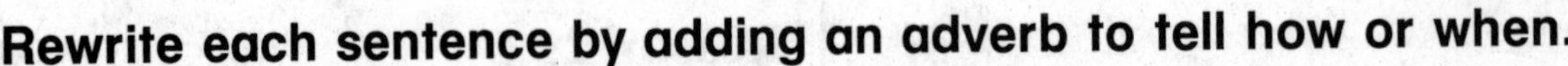

Rewrite each sentence by adding an adverb to tell how or when.

1. The family ate their meals together (when) ______________________.
2. Ginger stared (how) ______________________ out the window.
3. The log in the fireplace snapped (how) ______________________.
4. The family waited (how) ______________________ for a table in the restaurant.
5. The man went to the store (when) ______________________.
6. The girl (how) ______________________ wished for a for a bicycle.
7. He (when) ______________________ told them about it.
8. The dog ran (how) ______________________ past the house.

Name ______________________

Learning Word Match

Underline each vocabulary word. Then circle the word or phrase that is most like it in meaning.

Word Bank

miraculously
condemned
frustrated
communicate
restored

1. amazingly miraculously angrily
2. frustrated hopeful disappointed
3. complicated write or talk communicate
4. awarded doomed condemned
5. restored gave back took away

Answer these questions.

6. What might make you feel **frustrated**?

____

____

7. Name two ways people can **communicate.**

____

____

8. How would Helen's story be different if a doctor had **restored** her sight?

____

____

Name ___________________________

Problem-Solution Chart

Fill in the chart as you read the stories.

Story	What problem do the characters have?	How do the characters solve the problem?
Helen Keller		
Prairie School		

How are the problems and solutions in these stories similar?

____

____

____

____

____

Name ______________________________

Problem-Solution Checklist

In this theme you read about different kinds of problems and solutions. How well did the story characters follow the steps for solving a problem? Fill in the chart below. First read the steps. Put *yes* in the box if the character followed that step. Put *no* in the box if the character did not follow the step.

	Pepita	Poppa and His Family	The Quimbys	Helen Keller's Parents
Step 1: Think about possible solutions.				
Step 2: Make a list of pros and cons.				
Step 3: Pick one solution and see if it works.				
Step 4: If that solution doesn't work, try another one.				

Which character do you think was the best problem-solver? Why?

____

____

____

____

Name ______________________________

Prairie Word Search

Write the correct word on each line. Then find and circle all six words in the word search.

Vocabulary

sod fetch fidgeted prairie hauling trunks

1. Which word might you say if you want a dog to bring you a stick?

____

2. Which word names a mixture of grass and dirt? _______________

3. Dean was restless, so he twisted and turned in his chair. What did Dean do? _______________

A	P	R	A	I	R	I	E	U	T
F	S	P	A	C	T	E	B	Y	R
I	B	M	S	P	K	F	D	K	U
D	I	V	M	L	T	E	E	R	N
G	C	S	O	D	C	T	S	C	K
E	N	E	Z	O	R	C	B	O	S
T	L	R	N	A	Q	H	R	T	A
E	R	O	K	M	B	A	R	W	H
D	U	R	L	S	K	W	D	P	I
O	S	N	H	A	U	L	I	N	G

4. Which word names flat, grassy, wide open land?

____

5. If you are carrying heavy boxes, what are you doing?

____

6. Which word names things in which you can pack clothes?

____

Name ______________________________

Test Practice

Write a response to this prompt. Complete the chart. Then write your story on the lines below it and on page 222. Use the checklist on page 222 to revise your story.

1. A strange dog walks up to you on the street. He stands up on two legs and says, "Will you help me?" You say, "Yes." Write to tell what happens after you say, "Yes."

Characters	**Setting**
Problem	
Beginning **Middle** **End**	
Solution	

Continued on page 222

Name ______________________________

Test Practice continued

____

____

____

____

____

____

____

____

____

____

____

____

____

If you need more space, use another piece of paper.

Revising Checklist

- ✔ Does my story have characters, a setting, and a problem?
- ✔ Does my story have a beginning, a middle, and an end?
- ✔ Do I need more details? Do I need more exact words?
- ✔ Did I use clear handwriting? Did I fix any mistakes?

Read your story aloud to a partner. Then discuss your answers to the questions on the Revising Checklist. Make any changes that will make your story better.

Monitoring Student Progress

Comprehension Skill
Problem Solving

Name ______________________________

What to Do?

Review pages 406–407 from *Prairie School.* Then complete the Problem-Solution Chart.

Problem: Aunt Dora comes to teach Noah how to read, but Noah doesn't want to learn because there's nothing to read on the prairie.

Possible Solution: ______________________________

____

Pro: ______________________________

Con: ______________________________

Possible Solution: ______________________________

____

Pro: ______________________________

Con: ______________________________

Possible Solution: ______________________________

____

Pro: ______________________________

Con: ______________________________

Which solution do you think is the best? Why?

____

Monitoring Student Progress

Comprehension Skill
Making Generalizations

Name ______________________________

Saturday!

Read the passage. Then answer the questions.

Sam opened his eyes and looked at his clock. 7:30. Oh, no, he'd miss the bus! Then he remembered it was Saturday. No school, no reason to hurry. Sam grinned and burrowed deeper under the covers.

Finally, Sam got out of bed, pulled on his favorite jeans with the holes in the knees, and went to the kitchen. Dad was whistling and making waffles. Sam liked weekend breakfasts. He liked reading the comics while Dad read the paper. On weekday mornings, Dad left so early that Sam barely saw him.

"Do you think we could go fishing at Bass Lake today?" Sam asked hopefully.

Dad stretched and winked at him. "I don't see why not," he said.

Saturday was off to a great start, and there was still Sunday to come!

1. What generalization can you make about people's feelings about weekends?

____

2. What story details can you use to make your generalization? List as many as you can find.

____

____

3. What personal experiences help you make this generalization?

____

____

Name ______________________________

Divide the Words

Write the word from the box that matches each clue and draw a line between the syllables.

Word Bank

rodents	final
silent	below
lemon	clever
private	locate

1. at the end ____________________
2. animals such as mice, rats, and squirrels

   ____
3. intelligent ____________________
4. a fruit ____________________
5. underneath ____________________
6. quiet ____________________
7. to find ____________________
8. not public ____________________

Name ____________________

Find the Opposite

Read each sentence. Pick the antonym for each underlined word from the box. Write a new sentence using each antonym. Then circle each antonym.

Word Bank	
quiet	quickly
dirty	late
tame	answer

1. The turtle moved slowly.

____

2. Our new clothes were clean.

____

3. I need to ask you a question.

____

4. The campers woke up early in the morning.

____

5. It was noisy on the school bus.

____

6. The girls saw wild horses.

____

Name ______________________________

Spelling Review

Write Spelling Words from the list on this page to answer the questions.

1–8. Which eight words end with *er* or *le*?

1. ________ 5. ________

2. ________ 6. ________

3. ________ 7. ________

4. ________ 8. ________

9–14. Which six words begin like the word *asleep*?

9. ________ 13. ________

10. ________ 14. ________

11. ________

12. ________

15–17. Which three words begin with *be*?

15. ________ 17. ________

16. ________

18–25. Which eight words are contractions?

18. ________ 22. ________

19. ________ 23. ________

20. ________ 24. ________

21. ________ 25. ________

Spelling Words

1. I'm
2. ago
3. ever
4. around
5. wasn't
6. because
7. little
8. I'd
9. purple
10. again
11. shouldn't
12. November
13. about
14. aren't
15. later
16. apple
17. wouldn't
18. away
19. alive
20. summer
21. before
22. couldn't
23. behind
24. he's
25. able

Name ______________________________

Spelling Spree

Spelling Words

1. away
2. shouldn't
3. he's
4. before
5. November
6. wouldn't
7. apple
8. wasn't
9. aren't
10. purple
11. couldn't
12. behind
13. I'd
14. I'm

Complete the Sentence **Fill in the blanks with Spelling Words.**

1. My favorite color is ______________.
2. Thanksgiving is in ______________.
3. Let's have some ______________ pie.
4. The mouse ran ______________ from the cat.
5. Margo hid ______________ a bush.
6. I put on my socks ______________ my shoes.

Contraction Action **Replace the underlined words with a Spelling Word that is a contraction.**

7. I am __________ going to the game with Rico.
8. This is the team I would __________ like to be on.
9. He is __________ the best player on the team.
10. Our uniforms are not ______________ very clean now.
11. Last year I could not ______________ run as fast as Kara.
12. We all know we should not ______________ eat before we swim.
13. Coach would not ______________ let us skip practice.
14. The new game was not ______________ hard.

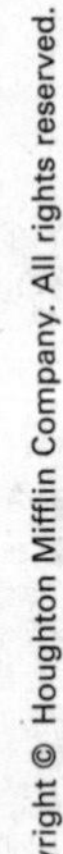

Name ____________________

Proofreading and Writing

Proofreading **Circle the five misspelled Spelling Words in this message. Write each word correctly.**

Playing soccer is better than hanging arownd. Being on a team is great becuase you make new friends. Two years aggo I was on a team. Now I want to play agin. It is abowt time for tryouts.

1. ____________________
2. ____________________
3. ____________________
4. ____________________
5. ____________________

Spelling Words

1. around
2. ago
3. again
4. about
5. because
6. summer
7. before
8. ever
9. later
10. little
11. able
12. alive

The Team News **Write the Spelling Word that means nearly the opposite of each underlined word or words.**

Our team practiced hard this 6. winter ____________________. We wanted to be ready 7. after ____________________ the first game. We knew if we 8. never ____________________ wanted to win, we would have to work. We ended practice 9. earlier ____________________ every day. We didn't just practice a 10. lot ____________________. We have put last year's season 11. in front of ____________________ us. Now we hope to be 12. unable ____________________ to win.

Write an Invitation **On a separate sheet of paper, write an invitation to a friend to join a team or club. Use the Spelling Review Words.**

Monitoring Student Progress

Grammar Skill Adjectives

Name ______________________________

Finding Adjectives

On the lines to the right of each sentence, list the adjectives. Then write each adjective in the correct column in the chart below.

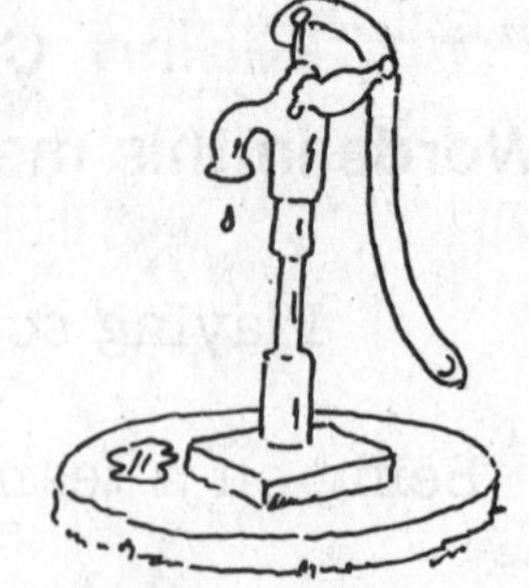

1. Anne Sullivan was a fine teacher. ______________
2. Helen did not like strict rules. ______________
3. The unhappy child would strike Anne. ______________
4. Anne and Helen went to an outdoor pump. ______________
5. Helen held out one hand. ______________
6. She felt cold water. ______________
7. Anne made patterns for five letters. ______________
8. The smart pupil understood. ______________

What Kind?	How Many?	Articles

Name ______________________________

Finding Adverbs

Circle the adverbs in each sentence. Then write the adverbs in the correct column in the chart below.

1. Noah went outside to fetch water.
2. Aunt Dora carefully wrote down the letters of the alphabet.
3. Next, she turned to Noah.
4. Then she asked him a question.
5. Noah answered sulkily.
6. He went out and did his chores slowly.
7. Aunt Dora cleverly showed Noah the value of reading.
8. Noah began to study willingly.

How?	When?	Where?
____________	____________	____________
____________	____________	____________
____________	____________	____________
____________	____________	____________
____________	____________	____________

Student Handbook

Contents

Spelling

How to Study a Word **235**
Words Often Misspelled **236**
Take-Home Word Lists **237**

Grammar and Usage

Problem Words **249**

Proofreading Checklist **250**

Proofreading Marks **251**

How to Study a Word

1. LOOK at the word.
- ► What does the word mean?
- ► What letters are in the word?
- ► Name and touch each letter.

2. SAY the word.
- ► Listen for the consonant sounds.
- ► Listen for the vowel sounds.

3. THINK about the word.
- ► How is each sound spelled?
- ► Close your eyes and picture the word.
- ► What familiar spelling patterns do you see?
- ► What other words have the same spelling patterns?

4. WRITE the word.
- ► Think about the sounds and the letters.
- ► Form the letters correctly.

5. CHECK the spelling.
- ► Did you spell the word the same way it is spelled in your word list?
- ► If you did not spell the word correctly, write the word again.

Words Often Misspelled

about
again
almost
a lot
also
always
am
and
another
anyone
anyway
around

beautiful
because
been
before
brought
buy

cannot
can't
clothes
coming
could
cousin

does
didn't
different
done

don't
down

enough
every
everybody

family
favorite
February
field
finally
for
found
friend
from

getting
girl
goes
going
guess

happily
have
haven't
heard
her
here
his
how

I'd
I'll
I'm
into
its
it's

January

knew
know

letter
like
little
lose
lying

might
morning
mother
myself

never
new
now

off
one
other
our

outside

people
pretty

really
right

said
Saturday
school
some
something
started
stopped
sure
swimming

than
that's
their
them
then
there
they
thought
through
to
today

tonight
too
two

until

very

want
was
Wednesday
we're
where
while
who
whole
world
would
wouldn't
write
writing

you
your

Take-Home Word List

Seal Surfer

Adding Endings

care– e + ed = car**ed**

save – e + ing = sav**ing**

wrap + p + ed = wrap**ped**

grin + n + ing = grin**ning**

baby – y + ies = bab**ies**

carry – y + ied = carr**ied**

Spelling Words

1. cared
2. babies
3. chopped
4. saving
5. carried
6. fixing
7. hurried
8. joking
9. grinning
10. smiled
11. wrapped
12. parties

Challenge Words

1. moving
2. libraries

My Study List
Add your own spelling words on the back.

Take-Home Word List

Animal Habitats Reading-Writing Workshop

Look for familiar spelling patterns in these words to help you remember their spellings.

Spelling Words

1. girl
2. they
3. want
4. was
5. into
6. who
7. our
8. new
9. would
10. could
11. a lot
12. buy

Challenge Words

1. wouldn't
2. world
3. through
4. while

My Study List
Add your own spelling words on the back.

Take-Home Word List

Nights of the Pufflings

The Vowel + /r/ Sounds in *hair*

/âr/ → **care, hair, bear**

Spelling Words

1. hair
2. care
3. chair
4. pair
5. bear
6. where
7. scare
8. air
9. pear
10. bare
11. fair
12. share

Challenge Words

1. flair
2. farewell

My Study List
Add your own spelling words on the back.

Take-Home Word List

Name ____________

My Study List

1. ____________
2. ____________
3. ____________
4. ____________
5. ____________
6. ____________
7. ____________
8. ____________
9. ____________
10. ____________

Review Words

1. buy
2. could

How to Study a Word

Look at the word.
Say the word.
Think about the word.
Write the word.
Check the spelling.

Take-Home Word List

Name ____________

My Study List

1. ____________
2. ____________
3. ____________
4. ____________
5. ____________
6. ____________
7. ____________
8. ____________
9. ____________
10. ____________

How to Study a Word

Look at the word.
Say the word.
Think about the word.
Write the word.
Check the spelling.

Take-Home Word List

Name ____________

My Study List

1. ____________
2. ____________
3. ____________
4. ____________
5. ____________
6. ____________
7. ____________
8. ____________
9. ____________
10. ____________

Review Words

1. making
2. stopped

How to Study a Word

Look at the word.
Say the word.
Think about the word.
Write the word.
Check the spelling.

Take-Home Word List

Across the Wide Dark Sea

The Vowel Sounds in *tooth* and *cook*

/o͞o/ → **too**th, ch**ew**

/o͝o/ → c**oo**k

Spelling Words

1. tooth
2. chew
3. grew
4. cook
5. shoe
6. blue
7. boot
8. flew
9. shook
10. balloon
11. drew
12. spoon

Challenge Words

1. loose
2. brook

My Study List
Add your own spelling words on the back. →

Take-Home Word List

Animal Habitats Spelling Review

Spelling Words

1. pair
2. unhurt
3. grinning
4. air
5. smiled
6. sadly
7. care
8. retell
9. babies
10. bear
11. unlike
12. cared
13. scare
14. hopeful
15. parties
16. pear
17. remake
18. chopped
19. bare
20. unhappy
21. joking
22. chair
23. friendly
24. carried
25. helper

See the back for Challenge Words

My Study List
Add your own spelling words on the back. →

Take-Home Word List

Two Days in May

Prefixes and Suffixes

re + make = **re**make
un + happy = **un**happy
care + **ful** = care**ful**
friend + **ly** = friend**ly**
help + **er** = help**er**

Spelling Words

1. helper
2. unfair
3. friendly
4. unhappy
5. remake
6. careful
7. hopeful
8. unlike
9. retell
10. sadly
11. farmer
12. unhurt

Challenge Words

1. unimportant
2. silently

My Study List
Add your own spelling words on the back. →

Take-Home Word List

Name ____________________

My Study List

1. ____________________
2. ____________________
3. ____________________
4. ____________________
5. ____________________
6. ____________________
7. ____________________
8. ____________________
9. ____________________
10. ____________________

Review Words

1. have
2. said

How to Study a Word

Look at the word.
Say the word.
Think about the word.
Write the word.
Check the spelling.

Take-Home Word List

Name ____________________

My Study List

1. ____________________
2. ____________________
3. ____________________
4. ____________________
5. ____________________
6. ____________________
7. ____________________
8. ____________________
9. ____________________
10. ____________________

Challenge Words

1. farewell
2. flair
3. moving
4. libraries
5. silently

How to Study a Word

Look at the word.
Say the word.
Think about the word.
Write the word.
Check the spelling.

Take-Home Word List

Name ____________________

My Study List

1. ____________________
2. ____________________
3. ____________________
4. ____________________
5. ____________________
6. ____________________
7. ____________________
8. ____________________
9. ____________________
10. ____________________

Review Words

1. good
2. soon

How to Study a Word

Look at the word.
Say the word.
Think about the word.
Write the word.
Check the spelling.

Take-Home Word List

Trapped by the Ice!

The VCCV Pattern
VC | CV
Mon | **day**
sud | **den**

Spelling Words

1. Monday
2. sudden
3. until
4. forget
5. happen
6. follow
7. dollar
8. window
9. hello
10. market
11. pretty
12. order

Challenge Words

1. stubborn
2. expect

My Study List
Add your own spelling words on the back.

Take-Home Word List

Yunmi and Halmoni's Trip

The Vowel Sound in *bought*
/ô/ → b**ough**t, c**augh**t

Spelling Words

1. caught
2. thought
3. bought
4. laugh
5. through
6. enough
7. fought
8. daughter
9. taught
10. brought
11. ought
12. cough

Challenge Words

1. sought
2. granddaughter

My Study List
Add your own spelling words on the back.

Take-Home Word List

Voyagers Reading-Writing Workshop

Look for familiar spelling patterns in these words to help you remember their spellings.

Spelling Words

1. down
2. how
3. its
4. coming
5. stopped
6. started
7. wrote
8. swimming
9. from
10. write
11. writing
12. brought

Challenge Words

1. favorite
2. sure
3. clothes
4. heard

My Study List
Add your own spelling words on the back.

Take-Home Word List

Name ______________

My Study List

1. ______________
2. ______________
3. ______________
4. ______________
5. ______________
6. ______________
7. ______________
8. ______________
9. ______________
10. ______________

How to Study a Word

Look at the word.
Say the word.
Think about the word.
Write the word.
Check the spelling.

Take-Home Word List

Name ______________

My Study List

1. ______________
2. ______________
3. ______________
4. ______________
5. ______________
6. ______________
7. ______________
8. ______________
9. ______________
10. ______________

Review Words

1. teeth
2. was

How to Study a Word

Look at the word.
Say the word.
Think about the word.
Write the word.
Check the spelling.

Take-Home Word List

Name ______________

My Study List

1. ______________
2. ______________
3. ______________
4. ______________
5. ______________
6. ______________
7. ______________
8. ______________
9. ______________
10. ______________

Review Words

1. after
2. funny

How to Study a Word

Look at the word.
Say the word.
Think about the word.
Write the word.
Check the spelling.

Take-Home Word List

Smart Solutions Reading-Writing Workshop

Look for familiar spelling patterns in these words to help you remember their spellings.

Spelling Words

1. his
2. I'd
3. I'm
4. that's
5. didn't
6. don't
7. know
8. outside
9. been
10. we're
11. anyone
12. anyway

Challenge Words

1. lose
2. finally
3. different
4. happily

My Study List
Add your own spelling words on the back.

Take-Home Word List

Pepita Talks Twice

Words That End with *er* or *le*
/ər/ → summer
/əl/ → little

Spelling Words

1. summer
2. winter
3. little
4. October
5. travel
6. color
7. apple
8. able
9. November
10. ever
11. later
12. purple

Challenge Words

1. thermometer
2. mumble

My Study List
Add your own spelling words on the back.

Take-Home Word List

Voyagers Spelling Review

Spelling Words

1. grew
2. daughter
3. until
4. cook
5. ought
6. forget
7. balloon
8. caught
9. dollar
10. boot
11. window
12. taught
13. flew
14. brought
15. hello
16. tooth
17. Monday
18. pretty
19. chew
20. sudden
21. order
22. spoon
23. thought
24. happen
25. bought

See the back for Challenge Words

My Study List
Add your own spelling words on the back.

Take-Home Word List

Name ____________

My Study List

1. ____________
2. ____________
3. ____________
4. ____________
5. ____________
6. ____________
7. ____________
8. ____________
9. ____________
10. ____________

Challenge Words

1. brook
2. expect
3. loose
4. stubborn
5. granddaughter

How to Study a Word

Look at the word.
Say the word.
Think about the word.
Write the word.
Check the spelling.

Take-Home Word List

Name ____________

My Study List

1. ____________
2. ____________
3. ____________
4. ____________
5. ____________
6. ____________
7. ____________
8. ____________
9. ____________
10. ____________

Review Words

1. flower
2. people

How to Study a Word

Look at the word.
Say the word.
Think about the word.
Write the word.
Check the spelling.

Take-Home Word List

Name ____________

My Study List

1. ____________
2. ____________
3. ____________
4. ____________
5. ____________
6. ____________
7. ____________
8. ____________
9. ____________
10. ____________

How to Study a Word

Look at the word.
Say the word.
Think about the word.
Write the word.
Check the spelling.

Take-Home Word List

Smart Solutions Spelling Review

Spelling Words

1. little
2. again
3. summer
4. alive
5. purple
6. around
7. I'm
8. able
9. wouldn't
10. ago
11. ever
12. before
13. aren't
14. I'd
15. because
16. wouldn't
17. away
18. couldn't
19. Novem-ber
20. shouldn't
21. apple
22. about
23. behind
24. wasn't
25. later

See the back for Challenge Words

My Study List
Add your own spelling words on the back.

Take-Home Word List

Ramona Quimby, Age 8

Contractions
A **contraction** is a short way of writing two or more words. An apostrophe replaces any dropped letters.

Spelling Words

1. I'm
2. he's
3. aren't
4. couldn't
5. won't
6. o'clock
7. wouldn't
8. weren't
9. she's
10. wasn't
11. I'd
12. shouldn't

Challenge Words

1. let's
2. who's

My Study List
Add your own spelling words on the back.

Take-Home Word List

Poppa's New Pants

Words That Begin with *a* or *be*
/ə/ → **a**gain
/bĭ/ → **be**fore

Spelling Words

1. began
2. again
3. around
4. before
5. away
6. about
7. alive
8. because
9. ahead
10. between
11. behind
12. ago

Challenge Words

1. awhile
2. beyond

My Study List
Add your own spelling words on the back.

Take-Home Word List

Name ________________

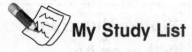

My Study List

1. ________________
2. ________________
3. ________________
4. ________________
5. ________________
6. ________________
7. ________________
8. ________________
9. ________________
10. ________________

Review Words

1. they
2. want

How to Study a Word

Look at the word.
Say the word.
Think about the word.
Write the word.
Check the spelling.

Take-Home Word List

Name ________________

My Study List

1. ________________
2. ________________
3. ________________
4. ________________
5. ________________
6. ________________
7. ________________
8. ________________
9. ________________
10. ________________

Review Words

1. can't
2. isn't

How to Study a Word

Look at the word.
Say the word.
Think about the word.
Write the word.
Check the spelling.

Take-Home Word List

Name ________________

My Study List

1. ________________
2. ________________
3. ________________
4. ________________
5. ________________
6. ________________
7. ________________
8. ________________
9. ________________
10. ________________

Challenge Words

1. mumble
2. let's
3. awhile
4. who's
5. thermometer

How to Study a Word

Look at the word.
Say the word.
Think about the word.
Write the word.
Check the spelling.

Take-Home Word Lists

Focus on Fairy Tales

Spelling the /s/Sound in *face*

/s/ → face, city

Spelling Words

1. face
2. city
3. pencil
4. place
5. center
6. dance
7. race
8. circle
9. nice
10. once
11. princess
12. circus

Challenge Words

1. silence
2. excitement

My Study List
Add your own spelling words on the back.

Take-Home Word Lists

Focus on Biography

Changing Final *y* to *i*

puppy− y + ies = puppies

Spelling Words

1. puppies
2. flies
3. stories
4. skies
5. driest
6. candies
7. pennies
8. cried
9. ponies
10. bunnies
11. happier
12. funniest

Challenge Words

1. easier
2. busiest

My Study List
Add your own spelling words on the back.

247

Take-Home Word Lists

Name ____________

My Study List

1. ____________
2. ____________
3. ____________
4. ____________
5. ____________
6. ____________
7. ____________
8. ____________
9. ____________
10. ____________
11. ____________
12. ____________

Review Words

1. tried
2. babies

How to Study a Word

Look at the word.
Say the word.
Think about the word.
Write the word.
Check the spelling.

Take-Home Word Lists

Name ____________

My Study List

1. ____________
2. ____________
3. ____________
4. ____________
5. ____________
6. ____________
7. ____________
8. ____________
9. ____________
10. ____________
11. ____________
12. ____________

Review Words

1. chase
2. size

How to Study a Word

Look at the word.
Say the word.
Think about the word.
Write the word.
Check the spelling.

Take-Home Word Lists

Problem Words

Words	Rules	Examples
are our	*Are* is a verb. *Our* is a possessive pronoun.	Are these gloves yours? This is our car.
doesn't don't	Use *doesn't* with singular nouns, *he*, *she*, and *it*. Use *don't* with plural nouns, *I*, *you*, *we*, and *they*.	Dad doesn't swim. We don't swim.
good well	Use the adjective *good* to describe nouns. Use the adverb *well* to describe verbs.	The weather looks good. She sings well.
its it's	*Its* is a possessive pronoun. *It's* means "*it is*" (contraction).	The dog wagged its tail. It's cold today.
let leave	*Let* means "to allow." *Leave* means "to go away from" or "to let stay."	Please let me go swimming. I will leave soon. Leave it on my desk.
set sit	*Set* means "to put." *Sit* means "to rest or stay in one place."	Set the vase on the table. Please sit in this chair.
their there they're	*Their* means "belonging to them." *There* means "at or in that place." *They're* means "*they are*" (contraction).	Their coats are on the bed. Is Carlos there? They're going to the store.
two to too	*Two* is a number. *To* means "toward." *Too* means "also" or "more than enough."	I bought two shirts. A cat ran to the tree. Can we go too? I ate too many peas.
your you're	*Your* is a possessive pronoun. *You're* means "*you are*" (contraction).	Are these your glasses? You're late again!

Proofreading Checklist

Read each question below. Then check your paper. Correct any mistakes you find. After you have corrected them, put a check mark in the box next to the question.

- ☐ 1. Did I indent each paragraph?
- ☐ 2. Does each sentence tell one complete thought?
- ☐ 3. Did I end each sentence with the correct mark?
- ☐ 4. Did I begin each sentence with a capital letter?
- ☐ 5. Did I use capital letters correctly in other places?
- ☐ 6. Did I use commas correctly?
- ☐ 7. Did I spell all the words the right way?

Are there other problem areas you should watch for? Make your own proofreading checklist.

- ☐ ______________________________
- ☐ ______________________________
- ☐ ______________________________
- ☐ ______________________________
- ☐ ______________________________
- ☐ ______________________________
- ☐ ______________________________
- ☐ ______________________________

Proofreading Marks

Mark	Explanation	Examples
¶	Begin a new paragraph. Indent the paragraph.	¶The boat finally arrived. It was two hours late.
^	Add letters, words, or sentences.	My ^best friend ate lunch with me t^oday.
(delete mark)	Take out words, sentences, and punctuation marks. Correct spelling.	We ~~looked at and~~ admired~~,~~ the mod~~d~~el airplanes.
≡	Change a small letter to a capital letter.	New York city is exciting.
/	Change a capital letter to a small letter.	The Fireflies blinked in the dark.
“ ”	Add quotation marks.	“Where do you want the piano?” asked the movers.
^,	Add a comma.	Carlton, my cat, has a mind of his own.
⊙	Add a period.	Put a period at the end of the sentence⊙
∾	Reverse letters or words.	Raed carefully the instructions.
?	Add a question mark.	Should I put the mark here?
!	Add an exclamation mark.	Look out below!

My Notes

My Notes

My Notes